MW00804012

THE
AFRICAN
DECOR
EDIT

THE AFRICAN DECOR EDIT

Collecting and Decorating with Heritage Objects

Nasozi Kakembo

Foreword by Justina Blakeney

ABRAMS, NEW YORK

To: Rafa Kalungi, Omi Jajja, and Opa Jajja

CONTENTS

FOREWORD

Art is a gateway to culture. In this book, Nasozi shares the colorful stories of artisans all over Africa—and invites us to look beyond the aesthetic appeal of "African design" toward the artists, makers, and stories behind them. I believe that when we bring old things and handmade things into our homes, we also bring with them the soul of the makers. These pieces have a vibe all their own. And that's because stories and traditions are woven into baskets and blankets, kneaded into bowls, and carved into furniture. Each maker is different. Each piece is different. Each story is different.

Whenever I travel I visit at least one flea market. I love old things and handmade things. I love chatting with the vendors (often artists in their own right) about the objects, where they were found and the lingering lore surrounding them. I learn a lot about people, places, and objects from a flea market. I feel a bit like an archeologist, piecing stories together like a fragmented urn. It was at my local flea that I first fell in love with indigo and mudcloth from Mali, Senufo stools carved from a single piece of wood, and recycled record beads from Ghana. But it wasn't until I chatted with the vendors about the pieces and then went on to do more research that I began to learn the traditions and meaning behind many of these things that add color to my appreciation, love, and respect for African textiles, furniture, and objet d'art. And of course, "African design" is not a monolith—it is not of one culture, or of one people, or of one style. Learning the history of, say, African wax prints, I learned that these fabrics are related to Javanese batik techniques. Learning these histories opens my eyes to how interconnected we all are—and how culture, design, and art are not static, but ever evolving.

As we learn more about the objects we bring into our homes, and the traditions and artists behind them, questions surface: Do we have responsibilities to the artists, designers, and artisans of goods that are now part of our homes? If so, what are they? Is it disrespectful to use these items in nontraditional ways? Who is "allowed" to bring these objects into their homes, and who isn't? What or whose languages should be used to describe these items? Who can and should sell and profit from these goods?

While no one person or book holds all the answers, I believe that the important thing is to start with the questions, the curiosity, and an open heart—and this book is an invitation for just that. We then learn about the objects, the people, the cultures, and we gain a more meaningful appreciation and connection with the things that adorn our lives and the artists who created them.

Creative exchanges like the ones Nasozi illustrates in this book play a vital role in increasing intercultural understanding, which can lead to empathy and inclusivity. And as we layer these pieces into our distinct homes and style them together with objects from our own traditions and our own cultures, we, too, become part of the story. Forever curious, open, learning, growing, piecing fragments together, and connecting the threads, to mold and weave together room for connection. ●

—JUSTINA BLAKENEY,
ARTIST, AUTHOR, AND FOUNDER OF JUNGALOW

INTRODUCTION

ABOVE *My mother's apartment in Büttgen, Germany, outside of Düsseldorf.*
OPPOSITE *My dad in Uganda on his graduation day from Makerere University. Left to right: An uncle, my father, Queen Sarah Kabeja of Buganda, my Jajja (grandmother), Nakazibwe Joyce.*

THE AFRICAN DECOR EDIT

I grew up in a home with groundnut stew for dinner and adorned with Senufo statues and Malian mud-cloth. My mother worked in an African art gallery in Georgetown, Washington, D.C., so there was no shortage of inventory in our home. She had also traveled extensively throughout West Africa by her midtwenties and obtained her own personal cache of West African textiles, jewelry, and art. These objects were a constant reminder of my connection to both people and places very far from where I was growing up.

English, German, French, and Luganda were spoken in my home, evidence of the many countries immigrant families often traverse in pursuit of opportunity, of freedom, or just plain peace. My mother, born and raised in the United States, sought refuge in Germany from the civil unrest of America in the 1960s. Already an avid traveler by her twenties, she quickly picked up German and French and befriended many African students who were in Germany studying medicine (as well as cultural activists, such as Miriam Makeba). This is how she met my father, who is Ugandan and was studying medicine in West Germany (after having also studied in London and Kampala). They eventually moved to the United States together, where my father was admitted to Howard University for yet more medical school. My family would eventually settle in the suburbs outside of Washington, D.C., and this is where my own story officially begins.

I didn't grow up traveling to Uganda. My father left Uganda as a political refugee in the 1960s, and the atmosphere was unpredictable for several decades afterward. Needless to say, he wasn't eager for me to visit for many years. Growing up among families who had found their ways to America under similar circumstances, it wasn't uncommon for many of my friends to have never seen the land their parent or parents came from. During college, I started to explore my Ugandan heritage more, and to define what it meant for me as a young girl of both Black American and Ugandan descent. To begin filling in that blank, I knew I had to get to Uganda right away! So one summer I simply told my dad that I wanted to go with him on his next trip. I wanted to meet my grandmother, Jajja (Luganda for "grandmother") Nakazibwe, in person. (We often "spoke" via the one phone in her village during holidays, usually Christmas and Easter, but mostly through my cousins because she didn't speak English.) I wanted to see the place where my father lived and went to school until his late twenties. A few months later, we were off to Uganda—I was nineteen. More than twenty-four hours and two airplanes later, through Rome and one night in Addis Ababa, and I was in Kampala.

One thing I found right away was that Africa did not feel foreign to me. It didn't feel "exotic" or any of the adjectives often used to gratuitously describe places in Africa and anything that comes out of it (people, objects, and otherwise). Granted, it was all very different than where I had grown up. But the things that

mattered were familiar—the presence of humanity. A stranger's smile. The melody of a bird song. The same stars in the night sky. The meanings of those things carry equal weight across the entire globe, and there are infinitely more things that unify us than separate us.

I remember one Saturday afternoon I was working at an artisan market selling my home decor collection in the Lower East Side neighborhood of Manhattan. The neighborhood has historically been one of the most ethnically diverse in all of New York City. Chinese, Puerto Rican, Jewish communities and more all converged in a footprint of less than one square mile. On this Saturday, my Ugandan baskets were on prominent display. In the short span of the eight-hour market, passersby from Colombia, China, and Afghanistan all stopped to marvel and share a story of how almost-identical baskets exist in their respective countries also. The elderly Chinese-American woman even explained to me that her grandmother used to weave these baskets when she was a small child in rural China. I will never forget these stories and how these baskets granted us moments, even if fleeting during Saturday errands, to nurture a cross-cultural exchange and understanding.

This book is an homage to my upbringing and my life's work, which would not be possible without the very skilled expertise and knowledge of the artisans and craftspeople throughout Africa. I've worked with traditional artisans living in more than a dozen countries

ABOVE *Mamoush and his family welcomed me to their home on the outskirts of Addis Ababa, Ethiopia (page 77).*

"I am going to take you into the lives, workplaces, and communities of sixteen traditional artisans."

in Africa. The stories are endless, and this book documents and shares artisan stories from a select number of countries based on the decorative items we find most frequently in homes in the United States and Europe (the largest consumers of such goods outside of Africa).

I am going to take you into the lives, workplaces, and communities of sixteen traditional artisans (see all the places I visited on page 13) who produce the very goods that adorn your own homes and sacred spaces. We will meet each one in their homes and workspaces to find out their story, how they became involved in the craft, and how this form of work has impacted their livelihood and opportunities. I want to tell the stories behind these traditional wares and found objects—the cultural story, but also the human story. We'll share meals with them, hear about their families, and learn how their craft has contributed to their sense of purpose.

While I generally introduce and describe objects based on their geopolitical boundaries, these "countries" are not particularly relevant when it comes to conversations about arts and culture in Africa. The languages, cultural traditions, and familial ties that predated colonization are still very applicable to daily life across the entire continent. Arts and culture don't adhere to the legacy of the Berlin Conference (where European colonial powers decided who would rule which piece of Africa), so hard lines between styles, materials, and objects do not exist. As a result, there will naturally be some fluidity and an organic exchange of influences and artistic traditions. I also use "Africa" as a geographic designation for this collection of fifty-four countries, and thousands more cultural identities; the way I use "African" is not an attempt to establish an overarching decor or design aesthetic, because I don't believe that one exists. I introduce you to the artisans through four decor categories: Furniture; Baskets and Accessories; Textiles; Walls and Floors. As many of the objects were created with another purpose in mind, the categories reflect the ways in which we incorporate these objects into our homes today, rather than their traditional use, though I do discuss each object's heritage and traditional purpose (one of the main reasons I wanted to write this book).

After we visit our artisans, we'll head to the United States, Europe, and back to Africa where families and community leaders welcome us into their homes and sacred spaces. I've selected a portfolio of home types and decor approaches that range from the homes of everyday people who happen to have an elevated or special taste to professionally designed spaces where we pull back the curtain on how the experts do it. These are all homes where people live, play, and work, too. African home decor can be integrated into all manner of homes and lifestyles, and the home tours in this book will show you how to incorporate or style African decor in your home in interesting and meaningful ways as well.

We'll visit homes in Brooklyn, Los Angeles, Accra, and Washington, D.C., to name a few, and illuminate the design principles behind each of their decor choices. Some of the residents infuse their homes with African objects as the central theme of their home, and some bring in African decor as an accent to another dominant aesthetic. Some have African ancestry, some do not. The common thread among them is that these are approachable spaces that tie in African decor for warmth, conversation, and character.

Lastly, I've assembled my best practices for shopping in the Ethical Sourcing Guide on page 16. So grab your design passport and we'll set out to meet the artisans and discover the inspirations that craft the found objects you love. ●

ETHICAL SOURCING GUIDE

The term "ethical shopping" has become an economic buzzword. Whether discussing fast fashion or Small Business Saturday, more mindful consumerism has been top of mind for millions of US households since the Great Recession. The pandemic reinvigorated the trend, and momentum for more responsible choices continues, with consumer concern expanding to include all manner of lifestyle sectors. But what does it really mean? This practice takes a very specific form as it relates to African found objects in home decor, and it is one that begins with addressing cultural appropriation.

Cultural Appropriation

We cannot talk about ethical shopping and African home decor without also addressing the role that cultural appropriation has played in how African artifacts came

to exist outside of Africa. Cultural appropriation happens when a more powerful group or person adapts or takes cultural characteristics from another without proper credit, compensation, or participation. The phenomenon has a long and well-documented history in Africa, although it hasn't always been known by this name. Cultural appropriation (and outright theft) of African goods has been routine practice for centuries.

Prominent museums, including the Smithsonian Institution, have drafted ethical standard policies in response to the demand for the return of cultural heritage objects that were unethically sourced. I have developed ethical shopping standards for patrons of African objects for the home at the retail level.

Whether you're getting acquainted with decor from the African continent for the first time or you've been a committed enthusiast for years, you might be wondering whether it is appropriate to make these objects part of your home if you don't have a cultural or ethnic

LEFT AND BELOW
The displays at the Choma Museum in Zambia discuss the traditional uses of Tonga-Binga baskets and stools.

connection to them. The short answer is yes. I am Ugandan and Black American (mostly of unknown West African ancestry), so I have a direct connection to much of, but not all, the African decor I have in my home and sell and/or create through my work with artisans (like Malian bogolan, or mudcloth). But I have educated myself extensively on the background of each, which is in large part what compelled me to write this book. There are ways we can all mindfully incorporate African decor into our spaces, and I introduce you to a brief set of guidelines below.

African Decor Ethical Shopping Framework

Rather than attempt to provide an exhaustive list of retailers where you can shop ethically for African home decor, as that is ever-changing, I designed a framework that will guide you in any city, on any continent, whether you're an independent shopper, interior designer, or a retailer. These four marquee points will help you shop more ethically—and for the design trade, source ethically—anywhere you are, including online:

Origin or Provenance > Maker > Seller > Description and Marketing

Origin or Provenance: Prioritize shopping as locally as possible. Independent and small retailers often work with independent vendors and suppliers and tend to place a high value on these connections.

- *Where is the item from, and why was it made?*

- *Can I buy this from and support a local maker?*

- *Is it a repurposed cultural item, or a new item that borrows inspiration from a traditional cultural object or design?*

Maker: Identify the maker and their connection to the object or influence—prioritize makers and brands who do.

- *Has the maker spent time in the country or community that the object is from?*

- *Is the maker benefiting directly from the sale of this item to me, or from me selling it?*

Seller: Prioritize sellers and retailers who have a cultural connection to the object.

- *Has the seller spent time in the country or community that the object is from?*

- *Can I buy this from someone connected to the cultural origin of this object?*

- *How is this retailer working with the community and people in the procurement process, if at all? If I'm a retailer, is this built into my business model?*

Descriptions and Marketing: Ensure that the description and marketing fully acknowledge the object's origin and story.

- *Does the product information provide relevant information, like what country the item is from, and the original name of the object?*

- *Is the object's name relevant to its provenance?*

I want to unpack this last point a little bit more, because it offers the first and most salient opportunity for awareness in the retail and design industry experience.

How we tell stories matters, so we should also be mindful of the terminology used to describe the object, and if you're a designer or retailer, the words you select to describe the object or influence. Some red flag words are "ethnic," "tribal," and "boho" or "bohemian." There are some that are far more troublesome, like "primitive," but we have largely moved away from that terminology. The trouble with these terms is that while they attempt to construct a design story, they achieve the very opposite by diluting the identity of the object.

Everyone has an ethnicity, so referring to anything as "ethnic" doesn't truly connect the look (or influence) to a people or place. "Tribal" can always be more specific by referencing the ethnicity or tribes. When it doesn't, it connotes something primitive and uncivilized. "African" is another favorite one. Africa is

Because African art and decor do not subscribe to traditional or classic European and American aesthetics, it gets thrown into the "bohemian" bucket.

If an item is produced in Africa, the ethical thing to do is provide its country or tribe of origin very prominently either in the name or the product description. Knowing the true origins of an object you bring into your home for the purposes of either making your life easier or amplifying your sacred space can only serve to make the work more meaningful. There's no ostensible downside to giving credit where credit is due unless the intention is to preserve a sphere of influence based on the narrative that these identities don't matter. It's time we move away from that.

Other Ethical Shopping Models

There are already a few models that spearhead this change on a macro level because it is of course much easier to shop ethically when the major retail players offer products that reflect the true dimensions of the world. Fairtrade America, which ensures collective bargaining, sustainability, and transparency of artisan-produced goods through a certification process, already does a lot of this work for us. But there is another theory of change that goes even further. By selling directly to the retailers and individual customers, a new brand of cooperative is removing the middleperson and retaining full ownership of the business side, from beginning to end. We'll meet one such social entrepreneur in Tangier (see page 228).

What I want you to take away from this framework is that our shopping decisions are currency, and chances are that if you picked up this book, you are already geared toward doing or wanting to know how to do that better. We all want to change the world in big and small ways, and we can do just that with information and our dollars. 🌰

a vast continent comprising fifty-four countries and countless more ethnic groups. Unless referring to multiple countries from around the entire continent, "African" is irrelevant. If an item or influence draws inspiration from Kuba cloth, for example, then it is Kuba-inspired (see more about the Kuba people on page 101). Yes, it is African, but it's from a very specific and relevant place and people within Africa. Granted, this all takes a little extra legwork and brainpower, but it's one small thing we can do as consumers and lovers of African found objects to correct the legacy of cultural appropriation and erasure. Turkish kilim and Japanese shibori are already integrated into our shared design vocabulary—we're well-positioned to integrate more origin-specific language when referring to African design as well.

Lastly, "boho" and "bohemian" are perhaps well-intentioned, but the terms belong to a cultural and artistic movement that started in nineteenth-century Europe.

16 OBJECTS AND THEIR STORIES

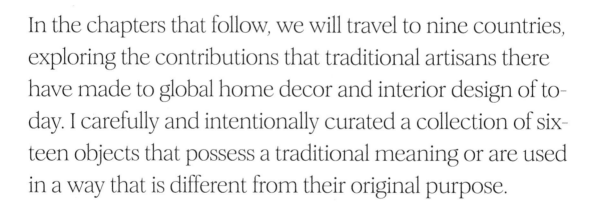

In the chapters that follow, we will travel to nine countries, exploring the contributions that traditional artisans there have made to global home decor and interior design of today. I carefully and intentionally curated a collection of sixteen objects that possess a traditional meaning or are used in a way that is different from their original purpose.

These objects transcend adornment because that's usually not why they were conceived. Each has a story to tell, as do the artisans who make them. These stories form the core to any meaningful discussion on craftsmanship in Africa and how it shows up in our homes—and our world at large.

FURNITURE

BASKETS AND ACCESSORIES

TEXTILES

WALLS AND FLOORS

FURNITURE

01

FURNITURE IS WHERE THE INTERSECTION of aesthetics and pragmatism are expressed most poignantly. Most (but not all) of the pieces were originally conceived as furniture in the daily, utilitarian sense. But sometimes they also tell us things, like how important someone is in the family. Or that someone has passed away and is going to be buried. We will see pieces that embody restrained minimalism as well as pieces that are intricately carved and embroidered as we travel to Morocco, Cameroon, and Côte d'Ivoire to meet artisans who create the treasures that have found a place in interiors far from where they are made.

OPPOSITE
Intricate doors and masks carved by Honoré Njuchingan.

LEATHER POUF, MOROCCO

SOUAD EL BAHIZ
●
Female leather maalem of Marrakech

ABOVE
The cooperative is tucked inside the winding alleys of Marrakech's leather district.

OPPOSITE
Souad's is one of the only (if not the only) female-founded leather cooperative in Marrakech.

SOUAD EL BAHIZ is in a league of her own. Born in Casablanca to a father who made his livelihood working with leather, she was never a stranger to this trade. But leather smithing in Morocco is a male-dominated profession, and it was not her intention to disrupt the status quo. As fate would have it, she later married a leathermaker, who had his own business.

Souad came to Marrakech in 1965. Her father wanted to expand his business and moved his family to Morocco's fourth largest city, known for its stylish riad architecture and interior design. Souad began learning to make different components of leather goods after she graduated high school, and she participated in the family business in a supportive role.

Maalem is the term for a famous maestro who represents the country internationally, and it, too, is a designation typically only extended to men. But Souad is a bona fide leather maalem, and she found herself at the helm of the family business after her husband fell severely ill. Souad stepped in to employ the skills she learned as a young adult and transformed her husband's one-man business into a full family-run operation, employing her brother and her son, as well as many others from the community.

She had been running the business for more than a decade when she met Rkiya Ibchine at a craft exhibition. The two women decided to go into business together and created a formal cooperative. Rkiya had a natural affinity for leather, and she started with the embroidery aspect since she already possessed that skill. She began to teach herself by deconstructing poufs and then putting them back together. She did the same thing with bags, and then added her own embroidery designs.

RIGHT
Goat leather, which is typically used to make the poufs, has a naturally supple quality.

ABOVE
Templates and patterns guide the assembly of various leather accents and accessories. Souad's younger brother, Nourrodin, was the first of her siblings to learn leathermaking.

Leather smithing takes and teaches patience, Souad tells me, and it exercises her brain every day. A pouf takes approximately two days to complete, and Souad also enjoys making modern designs that are in demand by younger generations, such as phone and laptop cases. She is heavily inspired by the era when all components of leathermaking were handmade. Today's varieties are not a significant departure from that model, but Souad can appreciate the origins of the craft that she now uses modern technology (like sewing machines) to produce.

As one of the only women in leathermaking when she started out, Souad faced significant challenges related to her gender in the early days. The men in the souks, where she sources her leather and other materials, were not accustomed to dealing with businesswomen as equals. This made price negotiations particularly difficult, and it took her a full year to establish the rapport needed to conduct this part of her business in the usual way. She is now a well-respected businesswoman who has traveled all over Europe sharing and exhibiting her leather goods as a representative of her country.

Souad and Rkiya started out with almost thirty apprentices. It takes three years for apprentices to earn an accreditation from a maalem, and many

of those who learned from them now have their own shops. Souad also formed a partnership with the government that sends girls who have dropped out of school to learn leathermaking from her and Rkiya. She points to her older brother, Nourrodin, as a profound inspiration for her to succeed in this role. Even though Nourrodin learned leathermaking before Souad, he is deaf and mute, and unfortunately this means that there are very few meaningful job opportunities for him in Morocco. Souad not only committed to hiring her brother, but to training and working with other members of the deaf and mute community. Her son Muhammed also works for her, handling logistics, communications, and banking. This is truly a family affair.

One thing that stood out to me in Morocco was that there seems to be a lot of government support for these industries, as I heard similar narratives from both of the cooperatives I visited there. The Moroccan government (the monarchy of King Mohammed VI) offers diverse forms of artisanal and small business support.

There are still challenges that Souad and Rkiya face on the business side. Because they are in Marrakech, close to the heart of the Medina, their rent is costly. But this is the best place for them to establish their brand, so they stay. It is also an accessible location for the people they teach. Souad wants to show more women that this line of work is not only for men. She says it can give more women financial independence. Souad also wants to sell to more shops directly. As Moroccan poufs are a well-established staple of African home decor, this is an attainable objective. Souad never intended to enter this line of business, yet decades later, she is shaping the future of her industry and community through her artistic expertise and humanitarianism, one leather pouf at a time. ●

HAND-CARVED STOOLS, CAMEROON

HONORÉ NJUCHINGAN

Master carver of Foumban

THE ANCIENT KINGDOM of Bamum's grand entrance is an apt prelude to the treasures that lie within its boundaries. After a six-hour drive northwest of Yaoundé, Cameroon's capital, I met with expert Bamum sculptor and woodcarver Honoré Njuchingan. The funny thing is, this meeting was intended and willed, but nothing was confirmed before my arrival in the West Region town. There was no set time. No appointment. My guide and I didn't even know exactly where we were going; we relied on word of mouth as we stopped along various points to ask taxi drivers and market women "where are the men who make the stools?" Landmark-laced directions ensued, which is still the most reliable way to get around all the countries I've been to in Africa. What we did know when we set out on our drive from the capital was that the historic kingdom of Bamum was the sole home of authentic Bamum stools, tables, and beds in the entire world, and we were going to find *someone* there who made them. Honoré would be that someone.

I met Honoré, who stands a regal six foot three, at his roadside atelier in the middle of a decorative woodcarving. I explained my work to him, and he was more than happy to indulge my line of questioning for the next several hours.

MIDDLE
Traditional Bamum stools sit in the foreground near the worktable.

BOTTOM
The studio is at the roadside headed toward Foumban's modest arts hub.

OPPOSITE
Honoré learned how to carve from his father.

RIGHT
*All work takes place
outside, and the studio
interior is reserved for
storage and display.*

BELOW
*Honoré has learned to
carve many different
items over his career,
including intricate
doors and masks.*

Honoré learned the art of woodcarving and sculpture from his father, and like him, he is also teaching his teenage sons. The indoor/outdoor atelier is a social gathering spot, or at least it was on this day. Not many visitors, Cameroonian or otherwise, venture to this part of Cameroon, and Honoré points to this as one of the main challenges he faces as a Bamum artisan. Authentic Bamum furniture still only comes from here, yet it is a remote location and artisans such as Honoré still rely on middlemen to buy their goods and sell them in the capital or export them. He also explained that the Ministry of Tourism does not necessarily recognize this as a legitimate field of work, so the area is not promoted as a tourist destination. This lack of recognition also inhibits him from obtaining bank loans or insurance, stifling his ability to grow his business.

Despite these challenges, Honoré proudly continues the legacy of wood-working, and in addition to teaching his sons, he imparts these time-honored skills to a group of sculpture apprentices at the Université de Beaux Arts de Foumban,

TOP
Just beyond the entrance to Foumban is the Royal Museum. The double-headed snake mounted by a giant spider is the primary symbol of the Bamum Kingdom, and it is commonly used in decorative motifs in Bamum art and objects.

LEFT
Various designs in the Hotel Zingana lounge in Bafoussam, Cameroon. A spiderweb design is seen in the foreground, which is central to the identity and pride of the Bamum kingdom. Depending on the size, each stool starts out as a single piece of wood, and each takes an average of one week to make.

RIGHT
*Carving a single stool
can take up to a week.*

BELOW
*The size of the tools
Honoré uses depends
on how fine the
carving needs to be.*

which has an alliance with its French counterpart. All the work remains handcrafted, as it was when Honoré's father taught him decades ago, and no machinery is in sight. The handmade quality is quite distinctive from machine-made counterfeits made in southeast Asia and Asia Pacific, which are then sold in national retail stores in the United States. But the discerning and knowledgeable customer will appreciate the irregularities that a human hand bestows—and that a machine does not. There's something special about a not-so-perfectly smooth finish that still serves its functional purpose while also keeping a tradition alive.

There are a wide variety of Bamum stool designs, and most of the decorative symbols possess cultural significance. The most common design found in America and Europe is that of spider webs. This theme then takes on various forms. Cow heads represent power, and elephants symbolize force. All of these motifs can most closely be described as a form of intricate latticework.

Depending on the size, each stool starts out as a single piece of wood, and each takes an average of one week to make. Artisans pour water on the wood as they go to soften it and facilitate carving, precision, and speed. The result is an enduring work of art. Traditionally, the stools were used to communicate social hierarchy: The smaller the stool, the less important the person seated on it. Important guests receive larger stools, as a sign of welcome and respect.

It is this tradition and cultural symbolism that makes Honoré so proud to share his work with people in places far from the grand entrance to Bamum. He believes the Bamum stools and tables have become so popular because of their undeniable beauty, and for him, the beauty of his culture cannot be distinguished from the vessels he creates. ●

THE AFRICAN DECOR EDIT

SENUFO STOOLS, CÔTE D'IVOIRE

ABOU SORO

Dalegué of Senufo

LEFT
Buildings are adorned with symbols of cultural significance.

OPPOSITE
Abou Soro became a master wood sculptor by apprenticing with his father.

KORHOGO IS LOCATED in the northern reaches of Côte d'Ivoire (also known as Ivory Coast in English), where it almost meets neighboring Mali and Burkina Faso. Côte d'Ivoire is a former French colony, and it's part of a group of countries commonly referred to as Francophone West Africa (hence its modern name). Over sixty ethnic groups called Côte d'Ivoire home, including the Senufo people, to which our sculptor, Abou, belongs. The ubiquitous African decor staple, the Senufo stool, comes from here, too, and I ventured to

Abou's workshop and his home to find out more about his life as a *dalegué*, the Senufo word for sculptor.

We met with Abou in Korhogo's Banaforo neighborhood. Neighborhoods are typically defined by their use, and the quarter where Abou works is considered the sculptor's quarter of Korhogo. The sculptors of Coco, as their neighborhood is called, play a key role in collectively maintaining the legacy of Senufo wood sculpting in this region. The dalegué of Coco are like a family because they continue to carry on the craft and

Dabas *in various sizes.*

because the craft is tied to family—they are all linked. Not only have they fostered a benign interdependence where each one has his own specialization, they also share the workload when orders are plenty.

Abou learned this skill from his father, and like other artisans such as weavers and blacksmiths, he is part of a caste that specializes in this industry—the skills are passed down through the generations.

Senufo stools and beds have found a permanent home in modern interior design and decor. The stools we incorporate into our spaces as a casual seating and tabletop option have been a Senufo fixture for centuries. But unbeknownst to many, Senufo beds are funerary objects used to carry the corpse during traditional processions.

Abou uses a *daba* (hoe) in multiple sizes to shape, add holes, and add detail to the sculpture. He then uses a *wonsougbor* (knife) for more specific details, to strip the wood and smooth it. Last, he uses sandpaper to finish. He seals the wood with polish. Despite the stool's popularity with customers, Abou's favorite item to carve is the *calao* (hornbill) because these are the special symbol of the Senufo people.

Bouts of political crisis and the pandemic have kept sales low for Abou and his fellow dalegué. However, they still manage to sell to local clients, including

RIGHT
A hornbill sculpture of this size, to the left behind Abou, can take weeks to make. Abou uses a daba (hoe) for all the carving.

local oracles who order masks for traditional practices. Gradually, local business owners and tourists are showing interest once again. Despite his children not being interested in pursuing this craft, Abou remains committed to passing on his knowledge to the community. Younger generations are taught by multiple sculptors, each specializing in different types of sculpture. Even older sculptors seek Abou's guidance for specific carving techniques.

While Abou has never left Côte d'Ivoire, he dreams of visiting France, the country that once colonized his homeland, and seeing the iconic Eiffel Tower. Until that opportunity arises, Abou's work serves as an ambassador of his culture, spreading the brilliance and influence of his Senufo heritage to the world. ●

ABOVE
Abou's storeroom displays the various types of woodcarvings he creates.

RIGHT
Senufo bed headrest detail.

ABOVE
Senufo stools come in various sizes depending on the person they are made for. Senufo beds are piled in the background.

LEFT
The Senufo stool's rough-hewn stage before sandpapering.

BASKETS AND ACCESSORIES

02

FROM INTRICATELY WOVEN PATTERNS to vibrant colors, today's African baskets and tabletop items not only serve as convenient and stylish decor objects, but also embody the intersection of Africa's artistic and utilitarian spirit. These traits are not mutually exclusive. Used for everything from beer making to gift bearing, traditional African baskets embody both beauty and practicality, telling stories of community, history, and the natural world. In this section, we journey to Uganda, Ghana, Zambia, and Côte d'Ivoire to explore the meaningful traditions and everyday activities that baskets represent and to meet the artisans who make them.

LEFT
A collection of Tonga baskets.

THE AFRICAN DECOR EDIT

EBIBBO, UGANDA

LEFT
Ebibbo used for my cousin Joyce's wedding at our family home in Mukono.

BOTTOM
The artisans (and some of their children) stand proudly with their finished ebibbo.

OPPOSITE
Agnes Musoke specializes in making the traditional baskets that Uganda is known for.

UGANDA IS HOME to a world-renowned basket-making tradition, which is also found throughout several other countries in the Great Lakes region of East Africa, such as Rwanda and Kenya. Traditionally used to carry gifts and dowry during wedding ceremonies, these baskets (*ebibbo* in Luganda, one of Uganda's widely spoken languages) have gained popularity as decorative home accents and are considered a must-have in any thoughtfully decorated home. Agnes is one of the stewards of this tradition and has made its preservation her livelihood and vocation.

Agnes has lived just east of Kampala, Uganda's capital city, her entire life. She is a wife and mother of six. It is from her home compound that she leads a cooperative of twenty neighborhood women, and occasionally her children, who she has both trained and employed as expert weavers.

TOP
Dried raffia is also used to make skirts for traditional ceremonies; this is a Baganda ceremony that my father attended in the 1970s.

ABOVE
Agnes demonstrates how she preps the raffia reeds for the ebibbo.

OPPOSITE
Biira holds up freshly dyed raffia before hanging it on the clothesline to dry in the sun.

When she was about twelve years old, Agnes learned how to weave from her older sister, and she mostly engaged in the craft at the time to earn some extra pocket money during her breaks from school. These skills are passed down from generation to generation as both a record of cultural practices and a reliable source of income. During our visit, her adult daughter, Biira, helps with gathering and drying the freshly dyed fibers as each batch is completed (think, studio assistant). Agnes is also teaching her teenage daughter how to weave.

The group of women that Agnes trained and works with eventually selected her as the group leader, a trend not uncommon throughout the African artisan world. Through word of mouth and tangible quality products, she gained a reputation for being faithful, trustworthy, and timely with paying collaborators. She also listens to each of their concerns or feedback, so they collectively decided that she would be the lead.

The workday is both a communal and intergenerational affair. Children jovially play among and between the mothers hard at work, while a jajja (Luganda for "grandmother") makes sure that they steer clear of any dangerous mischief. Agnes and her team draw their creative inspiration from collaborating and modifying common traditional designs. It can take up to two weeks for a newer weaver to complete a basket, and it still takes the more experienced women several days per basket. This is also why they complete large orders in groups, and why each basket is truly one of a kind.

Today's ebibbo making is both a traditional and modern affair. Agnes can harvest many of the materials directly from her own land. This includes the firm reed that forms the inside of each basket coil, the soft raffia that wraps each coil, and the dyes. Natural dyes are made from a variety of plants, such as hibiscus flowers and coffee beans. These plants typically yield natural browns, reds, and oranges. Large orders and

LEFT
Artificial dyes, which can be combined to produce a variety of different colors.

ABOVE
All dried raffia begins as this natural color before dyeing.

LEFT
Agnes boils and dyes the raffia on a homemade stove. The firewood produces a lot of smoke and heat.

OPPOSITE
The artisans wrap the inner reeds of each coil with colors, which are changed as the wrapping progresses to produce the different patterns and designs.

modern color preferences of customers abroad mean that some of the materials must change to meet the demand, including the use of chemical powder dyes that are imported from Kenya. Little else has changed though, and the organic and handcrafted nature of ebibbo still survives.

Typically, the cooperative's orders come from female independent shop owners from across Europe and the United States who Agnes meets while selling her goods at the craft market in Kampala, Uganda's capital.

Basket weaving has afforded Agnes and her family a steady source of income for generations. It has allowed her to put her six children through school, build her home, establish small grocery stores in her village, and donate some of her income to her church. She also appreciates the opportunity to work from home (and

for her team to work close to their homes), because this allows her to work while also fulfilling domestic responsibilities. (Agnes was dyeing raffia on one stove and preparing lunch on another during my visit!)

But the challenges that she faces now are beyond her control. With the changing weather patterns it is harder to produce ebibbo, which require ample sunshine for the dyed pieces to dry. Uganda has become cooler and wetter than it was when Agnes was a young girl learning how to weave, making it harder to coordinate her workload. There is also a new challenge—inflation. Rising costs of materials and transportation have a direct impact on her profitability. Despite the challenges, Agnes remains dedicated to her craft and expertise, and these developments make her story as an artisan all the more important to share and support. ●

BOLGA BASKETS, GHANA

LEFT
The hard straws are softened in water to make weaving easier, but they never break.

OPPOSITE
Atanga Adongo, tehese *weaver.*

THE BOLGATANGA DISTRICT in north Upper East, Ghana, rests in a vegetated savannah. This is where our Bolga basket weaver, Atanga Adongo, is originally from. His hometown is much closer to Burkina Faso and Togo (both culturally and geographically) than to Ghana's capital city Accra, which is on the Atlantic Ocean farther south. Accra is where Adongo relocated over two decades ago and runs his business.

Weaving has been Adongo's profession for decades, but Bolga baskets were not initially made to be sold, and I got quite a kick out of learning their original function. Bolga baskets derive their common name from their place of origin, but they are locally referred to as *tehese*. Bolga baskets were made to brew Pito, a local beer made from various cereal crops, during an annual festive season. Straining the mixture in the basket was the final step in the process, and the baskets were discarded following the celebrations. Designs weren't intricate but were made visually pleasing for the occasion. They were either left in their natural state or dyed with roots and a sand-clay found along specific rivers, which would yield a range of earthy colors.

Adongo learned how to weave baskets before he knew how to count money, he says. This skill was passed down to him from his grandparents, mostly through observation, but Bolga baskets were not yet made to be sold widely when he was still so young. According to local lore, a tourist saw the discarded baskets following the festival period, and taken by their beauty, asked if they could take some back to Europe.

LEFT
Each straw is split into two, until the very end, and then twisted prior to weaving.

BELOW
A custom lampshade created by Adongo for the Kokrobitey Institute (see page 166).

LEFT
A porch column at the residence and workshop of Winfulera is painted in the traditional motif of Northern Ghana. Winfulera is a Ghanaian businesswoman who runs a global shea-based body-care company from her live-work compound in Kokrobite.

ABOVE
*Adongo can make Bolga
baskets in many shapes:
This is the popular gourde
style.*

The visitor returned to buy more months later, and Bolga baskets made the jump from festive brewing instrument to global interior design staple.

Baskets are made entirely from dried elephant grass, called *kihkase* in the Frafra language spoken in Northern Ghana. The only time this is not the case is when leather handles are applied. Even then, the handle itself is constructed from the straw, which is then wrapped with leather. The grass straw that Adongo uses now in Accra varies slightly from what he used when he was still living and working in Bolgatanga full time. The straw found in this region is brighter, which he prefers, but it is not as long. Longer straws facilitate uninterrupted weaving, which can take up to one week for a large vessel, or closer to three days for medium-sized and baby baskets. Once sundried, each piece is split into two,

LEFT
*Both work and sales
are conducted beside
a busy road, next to
a few other furniture
makers.*

RIGHT
*I bought as many
baskets as I could
during my visit.*

with one side remaining intact. This allows for a secured double-strand twist and is what gives the baskets their durability.

Adongo draws his inspiration from artistry he grew up around in Bolgatanga. Homes there are painted in stunning geometric patterns in a way that reminds me of some of his work. He is also fond of the new ideas and challenges that his customers introduce him to. Modern chemical dyes, which come in a highly concentrated powdered form from Nigeria, have also expanded the scope of his designs.

He relies on foot traffic from customers en route to and from the market, and others driving by. He is located near several embassies (hence the order from the Dutch ambassador), so his workshop is strategically located.

Adongo also teaches others how to weave Bolga baskets, and his humble workshop belies the reach of his impact and ambition. Through a capacity building and handicraft training NGO he founded, he received an award for training eleven men in the Ghana prison system. He has trained hundreds of international tourists and visitors, mostly during a collaboration he had with the Kokrobitey Institute. His most famous pupil while there was former president Barack Obama (just before he became president).

Looking ahead, Adongo prays for large volume orders. This work is not just important for his own livelihood, but he still employs artisans in Bolgatanga when the need arises. Adongo and his brother Michael made every basket that I laid eyes on that day. There were too many to count. Adongo has nothing left to prove in terms of his ability and his dedication to seeing those around him succeed. If this is any indication of the possibilities that lie ahead, Adongo's prayers will be fulfilled. ●

THE AFRICAN DECOR EDIT

TONGA BASKETS, ZAMBIA

MARGARET SIANSAKA

Basket designer of Choma

I MET MARGARET SIANSAKA in the market town of Choma, Zambia, about a three-hour drive north of Livingstone. Margaret is a BaTonga (Tonga) basket artisan whose story begins almost one hundred miles away from the dry plateau that she has called home for forty years. Most of Southern Zambia, including Choma, is dry and semi-arid. This is a vastly different landscape than the one that the BaTonga people came from along the banks of the Zambezi River, which centered their way of life for generations.

In the late 1950s, 57,000 BaTonga were displaced when the British colonial government built a dam along the Zambezi River. This forced the BaTonga to relocate to what is now Binga, Zimbabwe. Zambia and Zimbabwe were not countries at the time, and as I mentioned in the introduction, these national boundaries are not very meaningful when it comes to African cultures. When the BaTonga were displaced up to hundreds of miles from their homeland, they carried their heritage and cultural knowledge with them—further evidence that cultural heritage in Africa transcends geopolitical borders. As a result, the baskets that Margaret has made her livelihood from are referred to interchangeably as Tonga and Binga baskets and are now also made in other parts of Zimbabwe as well.

Margaret learned to make *cisuo* (the Tonga word for "basket") from her mother. Although her own daughter wasn't interested in learning, she was able to teach her now twenty-four-year-old grandson, whose name is Obey. She also works with her daughter-in-law, who was with us during our afternoon together. She has been a widow since her kids were very young, and making and selling the baskets became a means of survival for her and her two children.

ABOVE
Fitzborn (left) from the Choma Museum was my guide and translator; behind Margaret (right) are her daughter-in-law, granddaughter, and son.

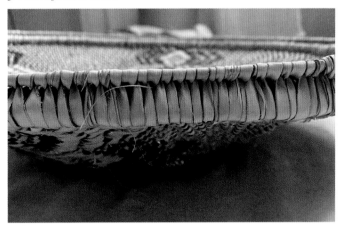

ABOVE
Coiled palm leaf.

OPPOSITE
Margaret's work in progress is as eye-catching as her finished products.

Southern Zambia's climate influences the vegetation used in the basket weaving process, and the most common Tonga baskets seen in home decor are still made from natural dyes and locally sourced materials. Tonga baskets are round with square bases and often decorated with woven patterns. A typical basket is made of palm leaves, while the bases can be made of reeds or sticks, providing additional support for the contents inside. Margaret works from home and obtains the *muyii* (bark) from trees in her yard. Muyii gives the baskets their rich brown hues, after pounding and boiling to extract the color. Margaret demonstrated this process in her outdoor kitchen, shaded by a tarp and thatched room.

Women are typically the basket weavers, although men are increasingly joining the occupation (like Margaret's grandson). A cisuo's size and design depends on its intended use, which could be for carrying dry goods or as dishes for porridge. When deciding which design to make, Margaret gets some of her inspiration from her training at the Choma Museum and Crafts Centre, and other times, the ideas come to her during the creative process.

Tonga baskets were not always made for commercial purposes, and it wasn't until the late 1970s that basket making became an artisanal trade, in part as a resettlement employment initiative. Because the women had been displaced from their previous ways of life decades earlier, they had to devise new opportunities for earning income, and the increasing interest in the baskets due to tourism was one way they could do that. NGOs and other organizations began to formalize women's groups. The Choma Museum, founded in 1995, has established twenty women's groups in

LEFT
Margaret pounds and boils bark from trees in her yard and neighborhood to make dye for the tan and brown accents.

BELOW
Preparing to place the palm reeds into the water for dyeing.

Beautiful Tonga cuuno (stools) are a staple in rural households for outdoor seating. This is where most of the gathering and work takes place.

ABOVE
These are baskets in the Choma Museum's storeroom, made by women from their twenty artisan groups.

TOP LEFT
A single basket takes, on average, one week to make.

LEFT
All the boiling and preparation take place in Margaret's outdoor kitchen.

seven rural districts in Zambia. Each group numbers between twenty-five and thirty members, and they come together depending on the demand and quantity of orders, which mostly come from Germany, the United States, and Canada. The members share roles and have administrative obligations. These cottage industries are usually home-based, such as Margaret's. Everyone participates in the collection of raw materials and preparation of the end products.

The women engage primarily in a wholesale relationship with the museum, and each is chiefly responsible for sourcing her own raw materials. Even though Margaret can harvest some raw materials right at home,

she still has to procure some of her materials (for example, she doesn't have enough land for harvesting all the palm leaves she needs). Rising cost of materials is one of the challenges she faces as an independent artisan, and this impacts the amount of money she can make.

Margaret is proud that Obey is also a weaver and has started working with an NGO in another part of Zambia as an instructor. Others in town have abandoned this work altogether for more lucrative jobs selling fruits and vegetables in the market, but Margaret holds optimism for the future of these wares. She believes that, over time, the young people will see the value in this line of work that also preserves their cultural heritage. ●

WOODCARVINGS, UGANDA

AMISSI KYEMO

Congolese woodcarver of Kampala

OPPOSITE
Amissi is skilled at all manner of woodwork. He hand carved this jacaranda bowl and salad servers.

ABOVE
The grinder is among the most important (and versatile) tools for this work.

AMISSI KYEMO'S REPUTATION precedes him. His woodshop sits in a two-story building overlooking a dusty road and a construction site. For the time being, he has an uninterrupted vista of the heart of Kampala in the distance. I happened to be on this road just a few days earlier and recalled the area, but not the building. There was nothing remarkable about it, but ascending a spiral staircase from the parking lot led me to not just a remarkable place, but an *exceptional* one. Although I had been working with Amissi for close to two years, we had never met in person, and hadn't even spoken. The finished products I always received did not disappoint, and neither did our visit.

Amissi came to Kampala, Uganda, from Burundi, and his parents are originally from the Democratic Republic of Congo (DRC). DRC is world-renowned for its woodcarved objects, particularly its masks and other cultural figures. Amissi's family carried this tradition with them to Burundi, and Amissi decided to formally study art and design in school. His father noticed that Amissi possessed a natural talent for art and design at a young age, and Amissi often helped his older brother, also a woodcarver, with ancillary tasks. He eventually left school to pursue this line of work full time.

Amissi utilizes both traditional and modern tools in his craft, which speed up his work and allow him a greater artistic license in his designs.

Amissi works five days a week, ten to eleven hours per day, taking off Fridays for religious observation and Sundays for rest. Custom requests invite him to experiment with new techniques and approach his materials and tools in a different way. But the rare antiques and vintage objects that his father

BASKETS AND ACCESSORIES, AMISSI

specializes in, and which he grew up around, are a constant source of creative inspiration. Many of these adorn his studio, and his father's shop just downstairs overflows with treasures from various ethnic groups in DRC. Amissi references certain aspects of these older pieces and brings them into this work in other formats.

His most important tool is the grinder. Its versatility allows Amissi to work with many different types of materials, including wood, horn, and metals. Still, he must use one of the most basic tools for the most durable woods, like ebony. For this work, he uses a *teso* (hoe).

One trivet takes three days, though it is hard to be precise because he makes multiple pieces at once rather than one trivet at a time. A bowl takes him one day to create, and he can also make five pairs of salad servers in one day.

Amissi has customers all over the world thanks to his international upbringing, tourists visiting Uganda, and family members who have settled in other countries outside of Africa.

Our own collaboration started more than ten years ago, when I sent a sketch of a trivet that I wanted to produce in Uganda and was referred to Amissi. After watching him transform the raw materials into magazine-worthy home goods, I can attest to the superiority of his command.

He makes local connections through word of mouth, and he is well known for his attention to detail and ingenuity. He creates custom woodwork for Kampala's booming hospitality industry and custom household products for the private residences of Uganda's elite class.

This line of work has afforded Amissi and his family a comfortable lifestyle. He has earned enough money to purchase land and build a home, and he has paid for several of his sisters to obtain their degrees.

But the challenges are also very real, and perhaps this is why Amissi does not wish for his children to continue this legacy. Woodworking is physically demanding, dangerous work. The tools require concentration

OPPOSITE
Amissi's dad runs the operational and vintage goods side of the business.

BELOW
This chair detail inspires some of Amissi's original work.

LEFT

The teso *that Amissi holds is the same tool used by his forefathers.*

LEFT

Amissi uses a wooden mallet and a chisel to carve each traced groove before setting the bone accents.

LEFT

Each bone accent is hand cut to the correct size and shape and set one piece at a time.

ABOVE
A trivet design that we collaborated on.

and precision, and any misstep can result in injury. Electricity outages in his neighborhood can prevent him from working for days. It is also difficult for artisans in Uganda to access financing to scale and invest in their businesses.

Despite these adversities, Amissi still acknowledges a place for this work in Ugandan society, and he would like to train his community's orphans in woodcarving and design. This idea came to him in the form of a dream, and he's already begun saving money for a new woodshop. In a larger space, he will be able to host training workshops that are, implicitly, about so much more than design-and-build. This craft is an avenue for math, building, and engineering skills—skills that will secure a better future for not just him, as we've seen, but for his community's most vulnerable. ●

TEXTILES

03

TEXTILES THROUGHOUT THE AFRICAN continent document and communicate histories and societal values. From Mali to Ethiopia and beyond, they act as visual legends to articulating one's status in society, purpose, or occasion. Meanings are woven into the cloth, both literally and figuratively, and serve to complement the oral histories that were once prevalent throughout most of Africa. Textiles were also often used as currency, and their intrinsic value continues to this day. We meet five textile artisans to learn more about their process and the meaning of this tradition to their community.

LES TISSERANDS DE WARANIÉNÉ, CÔTE D'IVOIRE

SORO NIBÉ SALIFOU

●

Traditional weaver of Korhogo

LEFT
It takes five to six days to weave a complicated pagne; simpler designs take two or three days. A single complex motif in any one of these mediums can take up to an hour to weave.

OPPOSITE
Salifou has memorized the equations that produce the patterns needed to execute these sophisticated designs.

SORO NIBÉ SALIFOU (SALIFOU) was born into a life of esteemed textile traditions. Born in the northern city of Korhogo, his birthplace is known for its imposing mud clay–painted figures on strip woven cloth. It is the capital of the Senufo people, where they live alongside the Dyula, who have a robust woven textile tradition that dates back centuries. The rural village of Waraniéné in Korhogo's outskirts is home to *les tisserands de Waraniéné*, the highly sought after Weavers of Waraniéné.

Salifou's father passed away when he was young. He moved to Waraniéné to live with his uncle, who is a Dyula weaver. When he was fourteen years old, his uncle could no longer afford his school fees, and Salifou started learning the Dyula weaving tradition, slowly becoming a prolific weaver and in-demand expert in his adopted hometown.

Dyula weaving is a centuries-old technique, passed down from father to son, or in Salifou's case, uncle to nephew. Nephews are considered "sons" in many African cultures, including the Dyula, so there is no word for nephew in the Dyula language. Your siblings' children are your children, and you are their parent, and so on.

LEFT
Salifou weaves in a covered outdoor structure that accommodates approximately one hundred weavers.

OPPOSITE
His carved wooden heddle pulley is both ornamental and functional.

RIGHT
The Kourouni (the wooden boat-like shuttle) carries the weft threads.

THE AFRICAN DECOR EDIT

Dyula means "trader" or "merchant" in various local dialects, and Dyula textiles were conceived of for mercantile purposes. They acted as social currency throughout West Africa for centuries before the French colonial era and served as proxies for wealth and prestige. Dyula textiles also became a key feature in the funeral rituals of their Senufo neighbors, where they indicated the rank of the deceased.

Dyeing is done locally, but raw cotton is now imported from neighboring Mali and Burkina Faso. Locally produced cotton was once a weaver's staple, but as Côte d'Ivoire focused on other major crops, small-scale farmers turned to other sectors, and now most weavers rely on imported cotton.

In addition to the finished woven strips, another remarkable aspect of the weaving process are the intricately carved heddle pulleys used on the loom. The ornate heddle pulleys' carvings resemble stylized animals or ceremonial masks, but in recent years the carved pulleys have been replaced by metal ones that are much more durable. Metal pulleys are made from bike wheel hubs, so while they're not nearly as attractive as their predecessors, they're just as ingenious.

RIGHT
*Foundational motifs
are combined and
reinterpreted to create
unique designs. This
one was commissioned
through an ongoing
partnership with the
social-impact brand
Five | Six Textiles.*

OPPOSITE
*The workshop and
showroom are part of
a larger community
gathering space.*

BELOW
*Less elaborate dresses
and pagne are more
popular with tourists.*

Each master weaver must perfect four foundational motifs of Dyula weaving, each one bearing resemblance to a comb, a diamond, a rope, and panther's teeth. Each motif is iterative, with both mutual characteristics and its own distinct look. Salifou is regarded as the most experienced weaver in this arena, and many other weavers in Waraniéné credit him as the person who helps teach many of the more complicated motifs. Weavers also seek his guidance if they are struggling to execute the motifs, as they know he has the design and technical expertise to find solutions to roadblocks. Salifou also teaches his younger brothers after school and during their holidays.

Today's Dyula weavers honor the aesthetic foundations of the practice, but each is also free to interpret and create their own original designs from that basis. Salifou especially loves weaving *pagne* (large cloth wrappers), and his artistic intuition steers him through the complicated motifs.

Intricate textiles are naturally more expensive, so they are made-to-order and not on display in Salifou's showroom. Tourists, both Ivorian and European, lean toward the simpler and less elaborate (and traditional) designs, so he reserves those for the showroom in Waraniéné where they shop. ●

THE AFRICAN DECOR EDIT

DORZE WEAVINGS, ETHIOPIA

MAMOUSH GOUZDA
●
Weaver of Shiro Meda

OPPOSITE
Mamoush stands proudly with one of his finished pieces for Bolé Road Textiles.

LEFT
Shiro Meda means "chickpea plateau or meadow." It takes its name from the crop that once blanketed these hills.

AT THE FOOTHILLS of the Entoto Mountains, just before the literal outskirts of Addis Ababa (Addis), Ethiopia's capital, is a bustling market neighborhood that is home to a vast array of Ethiopian textiles. Called Shiro Meda, it is the commercial and artistic epicenter of Ethiopia's traditional weaving industry. This is where I spent several days with Mamoush, an expert weaver who comes from Ethiopia's Dorze ethnic group, based in the country's southern Gamo highlands. Dorze weavers are known for their masterful weaving skills, and they now dominate the ancient weaving industry in Ethiopia.

Mamoush invited me to his home in a hilly section of the neighborhood, about a ten-minute walk from where he works. Mamoush's wife, Werder, greeted us, along with their one-year-old daughter Maramauit. They welcomed me in classic Ethiopian tradition, with fresh *buna* (coffee) roasting just outside of their home. There hadn't been electricity since the day before, but that didn't stop us from having a vibrant conversation.

Like most Dorze weavers, Mamoush learned to weave from his father, first helping with small aspects and eventually graduating to complete a *shema* (the traditional cloth). He learned by watching and by listening, as is customary with imparting traditional knowledge in Ethiopia and many other parts of Africa. Weaving is reserved for the men (exclusively until recently), while the women harvest, spin, and sell the cotton. He now belongs to a collective of weavers, all of them Dorze, that was formed as part of an investment and employment initiative sponsored by the mayor. They share the workload and profits, and even had a meeting to discuss how they were going to share Mamoush's compensation for being part of this book.

The men in this collective all have similar stories—they inherited knowledge from their fathers or grandfathers and came to Addis for better job opportunities. The process has not changed much from the days when their fathers taught them how to weave. The loom that Mamoush works on (called a *shimana*) is imported, but

ABOVE
Fresh coffee brews in this beautifully made jebena.

RIGHT
Werder roasts coffee beans in the outdoor kitchen area.

it mimics the traditional wooden loom that he learned on as a young adult. Other essential instruments are the *mekina* and *gari* (spinning wheels), the *khessum* (bobbin), *mewerwerya* (shuttle), and the *melkemiya* (shed sticks).

Ethiopian textiles are made to be worn, and the name of the attire depends on the size, purpose, and border design. *Kemi* refers to a dress or robe and is worn during Ethiopia's many Orthodox Christian holy days and other important ceremonies and celebrations, such as weddings. This is always accompanied by a veil-like *netela* (scarf) for the head, neck, and shoulders. The more religiously devout always wear traditional clothing. The colorful designs that many modern home decor styles draw their inspiration from is called the *tibeb*, which is the colorful embroidery adorning the edges and the center of the cotton.

When completing a custom design, the men review a picture and specifications once, and then proceed to weave virtually from memory. I observed Mamoush weaving during our visit, and at no point did he refer to a drawing or instructions. When creating original work, it flows from their own sense of artistry as if they are freestyle drawing, except on a loom. Both methods require a high level of concentration, and I was further astonished that they were woven in an "upside down" manner—meaning the reverse side faces the weaver, and the final design is not visible until the piece is complete and turned over. The results are impeccable and visually outstanding, with each piece taking up to one week to complete. Most of their orders come from local customers, and their largest orders come from Hana Getachew of Bolé Road Textiles (see page 141), whose mother used to have dresses made by the collective. Mamoush would like more large orders like Hana's, but the collective lacks the infrastructure for sustained marketing, logistics, and communication that kind of growth would require.

ABOVE
The compound where Mamoush works consists of eight massive building blocks, each housing different types of factories.

RIGHT
Mamoush, his colleagues, and me.

LEFT
Finished textiles for pillows, table runners, and napkins are hung to dry after a final rinse.

BELOW
The mekina *and* gari *(spinning wheels) have been made from the same materials for centuries.*

Mamoush is proud to be a weaver, but in addition to the workflow, he faces the usual set of challenges that accompany artistic work: Benefits are not included in his earnings and many other jobs possibly pay more.

Counterfeits are a new and modern challenge. Chinese factories now attempt to imitate the intricate and delicate styles of the *shema* and sell them for lower prices. But the discerning eye can easily note the difference. Apart from the subtle variations of handmade textiles, the work of Mamoush and his fellow weavers is further distinguished by their material: Authentic Ethiopian textiles are made from 100 percent locally sourced cotton, while the machine-made counterfeits are made from polyester and lower-quality yarns.

On the day after we first met, Mamoush went to pick up his son Nathaniel from home during his lunch break and brought him back to the work studio. Nathaniel proudly sat at his father's loom, smiling widely and imitating the gestures he has grown up around, not yet aware that the hopes and dreams his dad has for him look nothing like his own. The cultural pride around these textiles is undisputed, but only time will tell whether it's enough to encourage future generations to continue the legacy as a viable way of life. ●

RIGHT
Kemis and netelas *are worn during a wedding ceremony in Ethiopia's northern Tigray region.*

BELOW
This work takes high levels of con-centration, and the studio is mostly quiet throughout the day.

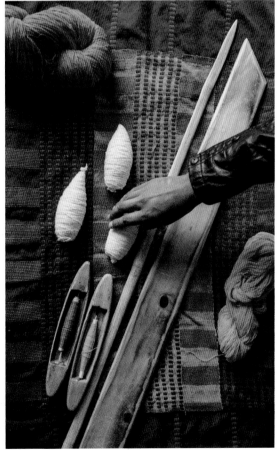

RIGHT
The number and sizes of the melkemiya (shed sticks) determines the intricacy of the design.

BAULÉ, CÔTE D'IVOIRE

OPPOSITE
Chris makes all the Baulé cloth carried in his shop in line with its signature warping and embellishments.

LEFT
Zaouli dancer wears a Baulé pagne as a cape.

AMANI CHRISTIAN-LOPEZ (CHRIS) is a master weaver in the village of Aguibri, Côte d'Ivoire. It takes at least ten years to become a master weaver; by that measure, Chris has achieved the title many times over. He began weaving as a teenager, learning from his father as is the tradition. (The skill is passed down from father to son, or from a male figure in the community. As such, all of Chris's brothers are also weavers.)

Chris was born in Yamoussoukro, which is home to the largest church in the world, the Basilica of Our Lady of Peace.

The cloth wraps (*pagne*) that Chris specializes in are commonly referred to as Baulé, which is the name of the ethnic group that he belongs to. The Baulé people migrated from the Ashanti region of neighboring modern-day Ghana, and they are direct descendants

TOP
Positioning the standing loom.

BOTTOM
The full length of the warp threads is laid out and carefully measured before being bound in the dyeing pattern.

OPPOSITE
A complete pagne has about ten even strips, and measures approximately 40 by 57 inches. Each strip is about four inches wide.

of the Akan people who still reside there. The Akan are renowned weavers as well, and the Baulé, which they were later called, carried aspects of this trait with them to their new land. Centuries later, Baulé textiles have assumed a rightful place in home decor and among the fashion forward outside of Côte d'Ivoire.

Baulé fabric was (and is) made to be worn during ceremonies such as weddings, funerals, and societal initiations, but it has also been adopted for contemporary use in skirts and full-length tunics. The adaptation of this cloth to modern life in Côte d'Ivoire suggests that it is now appropriate to use Baulé cloth in new ways, but understanding its full history and sourcing it from an ethical seller who adheres to principles of our Ethical Shopping Framework are essential when honoring this object in your home.

The instruments and process for making Baulé have remained almost entirely unchanged over the centuries, but a lot has changed as it relates to cotton. Before the French colonial era, which lasted almost seventy years, cotton was exclusively grown, harvested, and homespun by women. The colonial economy shifted cotton from a small-scale crop for personal use and local trade to one for export. It simultaneously introduced textile factories that produced machine-made thread and textiles. As a result, more weavers started buying machine-made threads, as small-scale production became less profitable. Traditional Baulé pagne have become more valuable and further distinguished for their ritual function, especially in comparison to the local mass-produced textiles brought about during the colonial era.

RIGHT
Because the ikat pattern relies on the repeated variation of dyed thread, the loom and the threads must be absolutely synchronized

BELOW
Warp threads are tightly bound with cloth strips before being dyed in indigo.

ABOVE
Pagne detail.

OPPOSITE
Chris's shop displays the breadth of his talents.

Baulé people have likely been weaving since the precolonial era (there is some debate about this, given the Baulé's itinerant origins), but they learned ikat resist-dyeing techniques from the neighboring Dyula/Guro people in the mid-twentieth century. With slight modifications to the loom (for example, Baulé weaving is performed upright, while others are typically seated), they have defined their own aesthetic. Baulé fabrics are dyed and woven in the ikat method, which means that the primary design is established by the variation of the thread itself. Embroidered accents in pops of bright, sometimes neon, colors delightfully contrast the indigo and white base, though this is a more modern addition. Once the individual strips are complete, each is sewn together at the edge, though not overlapping. The entire process takes about four days.

Chris maintains that the work is easy, but the process itself takes immense concentration and precision. Any deviation from the measurements will spoil the Baulé's iconic variations and render something else entirely. Chris says he draws his creative inspiration from God. Other times, he takes cues from designs and patterns he sees worn around him. He sells predominantly to women, who purchase the pagne to be worn as wraps, and he occasionally sells to tourists.

Chris is keen on continuing the weaving tradition that was passed down to him. He plans on teaching his sons when they're old enough, but for now, Chris teaches children from nearby villages. The next generation of weavers is already learning and safeguarding this tangible effect of the Baulé people's cultural values. ●

THE AFRICAN DECOR EDIT

BATIK, GHANA

ANGELA AFFUL

Resident batik artisan at Kokrobitey Institute, Kokrobite

TOP
Batik on the final drying line.

BOTTOM
Chamil Madhawa, Kokrobitey Institute's production manager, demonstrates how to create the stencil needed for my foam blocks.

OPPOSITE
Angie joined me at the Kokrobitey Institute five years after my batik residency with her.

I FIRST MET ANGELA, who I affectionately call Angie, during my batik residency at the Kokrobitey Institute (KI). At the time, I was an overly ambitious designer who wanted to learn batik and produce an entire collection in the span of ten days. Angie was my knowledgeable and forgiving instructor. Five years later, I returned to the Institute as a writer-in-residence, and although Angie had moved on, her work with batik has marked both her story and mine in an indelible way.

Angie came to the oceanside fishing town of Kokrobite when she was just twenty-four years old. Now in her early thirties, she is one of the youngest artisans in this book, and she straddles the new and the old generations of Ghana's traditional batik-makers. She began learning batik (a wax-resist stamping and dyeing technique) as part of the overall program at a vocational school in Accra. Soon after graduation, she came to the Kokrobitey Institute. Initially hired as a sewist, she was soon promoted to resident expert.

The origins of batik in Ghana, and in Africa more broadly, are curious. All oral accounts and historical literature on the topic point to the Dutch East India Trading Company of the seventeenth and eighteenth centuries as the origin (and this is the history that Angie also recounts). Wax had been a key component in highly sophisticated art and object forms in Africa for hundreds of years prior to European arrival, so I see this as an opportunity for further investigation. But for the time being, and as the stories go, batik originated in Indonesia and was brought to Ghana by the Dutch.

Ghanaians were fond of those styles and adapted the techniques to suit their own tastes. Batik became a common home and fashion textile all over Ghana, but the local demand and interest decreased over time. Interest from visitors and tourists remains strong, but Angie ultimately pivoted to a new career path because she did not have a channel to sell consistently to these buyers.

The work is tedious, and handling the hot wax is dangerous. Starting with six yards of fabric, usually cotton, the entire process takes two days if you are an expert and follow the steps uninterrupted. There are easily fifteen discrete steps involved in making batik, and they must be completed in a particular order to achieve the finished product and desired design.

The first step is to create your stamps. Traditionally (and occasionally today), stamps are carved from soft wood. We carved our stamps from discarded high-density foam, which is now a common practice. You then lay the fabrics on the table while melting the wax, which comes in large blocks and must be broken down into smaller chunks to fit into the iron pot. Then, stamping begins. The amount of time spent stamping depends on the size of the stamp and the cloth, but on average, it takes thirty minutes for six yards. The remaining ten steps include a series of soaking the plain cloth so that it can better absorb the dyes, carefully measuring the dyes to achieve the desired color(s), and dipping the cloth in hot water to melt the wax off (and repeating all this again if your design calls for multiple patterns and colors).

ABOVE
Natural dyes are made from fruits, vegetables, and herbs, including ground avocado seed, which is shown here.

OPPOSITE, TOP
Excess melted wax must be removed from the block before stamping.

OPPOSITE, BOTTOM
A stamped cloth soaks before dyeing.

RIGHT
The wax block is stamped in a repetitive (or sometimes random) pattern until the cloth is full.

OPPOSITE
The cloth must be rotated in the dye every five minutes so the color will be even.

LEFT
It takes about fifteen minutes to absorb the dye.

The art of batik has undergone various changes since its introduction. In addition to the stamps, another major change is the introduction of artificial chemical dyes. Angie learned to work with these alongside the organic ones, and each has its advantages and disadvantages. Artificial dyes require harsh chemicals, so you have to wear protective gloves while working due to the threat of toxicity and poisoning. The upside is that the dyes go a long way and artisans also have access to a wider range of colors. Meanwhile, natural dyes are toxin free and relatively affordable. The challenge with natural dyes is that they require a lot of raw material to get enough concentrated dye. Artificial dyes provide a shortcut, especially when creating large orders.

What I appreciate about Angie's journey is that it represents the accelerator that artisanal work can be. Not every artisan is obligated to stay in their respective line of work forever, and this can be a legitimate pathway to other endeavors. Angie's work and exposure at the Kokrobitey Institute afforded her the opportunity to explore other pursuits. She was able to teach batik to artisans and students from all over the world, one of her favorite parts of the job, and she was able to save enough money to start a family and then start her own small business. Angie opened her boutique, called Annie Luv Collections, just a couple of months before my visit. She also wants to expand the space so that she can begin teaching others again, especially the youth of Kokrobite.

BOGOLANFINI, MALI

BOUBACAR DOUMBIA

●

Legendary Bogolan pedagogue of Ségou

TOP
An apprentice creates an original bogolan design using a paintbrush.

BOTTOM
Apprentices learn the craft for up to two years.

OPPOSITE
Boubacar Doumbia is the founding artist behind Le Ndomo.

ONE OF THE MOST internationally revered, ubiquitous, and imitated African textiles originates in Mali, West Africa. Known for its endless combination of geometric patterns and earth tones, some of us refer to this textile as mudcloth. Others know it as bogolanfini or bogolan. The English term (mudcloth) succinctly encapsulates this cloth's origin, process, and composition: *Bogo* means "earth" or "mud'; *lan* means "with"; and *fini* means "cloth." And thus you have bogolanfini, a Bamana word, which I refer to as bogolan in our discussion.

When I started my home decor journey, bogolan was one of the first textiles I worked with. I received an assortment, both contemporary and vintage, from my mother. Living in Bedford-Stuyvesant, Brooklyn, Mali did not, in fact, feel very far away. Many of my neighbors were from Mali and its neighboring countries. But this proximity simultaneously created a dissonance that I wanted to resolve, which led me to Pélengana. Pélengana is in the Ségou region of Mali, and is home to master bogolan artist, Boubacar Doumbia.

Boubacar is Malinké, a subgroup of the Mandinka people who live throughout present day Mali, Senegal, and Côte d'Ivoire. Bogolan is unique to the various ethnic groups (including the prolific Bamana), and authentic bogolan is only produced in this corner of the world. Boubacar learned the art of bogolan as a student at the Institut National des Arts, and later founded Groupe Bogolan Kasobané with five fellow students in 1978. Kasobané is a collective that promotes the preservation of natural dyes in bogolan production; the group pioneered the exploration of traditional bogolan techniques on contemporary mediums.

Boubacar later established the Ndomo Center (Le Ndomo) in 2004 in Pélengana, on the banks of the Niger River, where cotton and other raw materials are plentiful. Mali was facing an exodus of its best and brightest to Europe due to economic uncertainty, and Boubacar committed to stopping the brain drain. Le Ndomo trains young job seekers and artists in local cotton and natural dyeing techniques as a lever for cultural, economic, and social development. Boubacar and Le Ndomo's master weavers train young people from all different areas and ethnic groups of Mali, starting as young as eighteen years old. The collective completes large orders, and individual work also happens onsite. Members share 10 percent of their profits and set up savings accounts as part of their life skills and business training.

Bogolan dates back to the tenth century, and production was once an exclusively female-led activity. Men wove the cloth, but the art and adornment rested squarely in the domain of women and girls, and every piece told a story. Traditional symbols and motifs conveyed societal values using visual proverbs, and themes often related to peace in the family and the community. The female garment wearer acted as a messenger, intentionally broadcasting these values wherever she went, and symbols were passed from mother to daughter.

Bogolan was traditionally worn by hunters, pregnant or menstruating women, or anyone in danger of losing blood; it is believed that the meandering motifs would confuse the enemies and spirits, and the close weave of the fabric would protect the wearer's body. Bogolan is now fully integrated into Malian popular culture and is worn as everyday attire by many. The most meaningful symbols are said to remain safeguarded by bogolan's culture and producers. Le Ndomo prides itself on the creation of both traditional bogolan that preserve these meanings and contemporary designs that preserve the process.

Both men and women produce bogolan today, and Le Ndomo (and most bogolan artisans) still use 100 percent natural dyes. The process for affixing the dyes to the cloth cannot be done in any other way. Bogolan begins with about seven cotton strips woven on a traditional loom. Each measures about six inches wide, and they are sewn together, edge to edge, creating one piece of medium to large cloth.

The natural dye is first extracted from the leaves and bark of the ngalama tree, which is rich in tannin that has fixative properties. The leaves and bark are soaked and boiled, and once the plain cotton is bathed in the solution, it is put out in the sun to dry.

Next, Le Ndomo artisans collect mud clay from exposed areas of the Niger riverbank and bed and store it in large vessels where it ferments. The mud is rich in iron, and the longer it ferments, the stronger the dye reaction will be. The artist distributes the mud for the first layer of designs, and the reaction with the tannin gives bogolan its black and various other earth-toned pigments. The quantity of mud and sequencing of each step are all part of the knowledge that Boubacar shares with the trainees at Le Ndomo.

The final step "bleaches" out the base pigment and allows the white designs to emerge. Liquified natural soap made from shea butter and wood ash is hand drawn or stenciled onto the pigmented cloth in the desired patterns and then left in the sun for a few more days before being washed off. What remains are the colorfast, iconic contrasting designs that have popularized bogolan in home decor and interior design across the globe.

It can take a well-seasoned artist weeks to complete, so today's artisans have innovated around speed. Bleach and non-natural soaps are sometimes used in small amounts to speed up the drawing step, but it still only works once it is added to the organic mixture. Stencils are also a recent drawing tool, but, traditionally, artisans would draw freehand (and sometimes still do).

Bogolan will continue to flourish as a tangible cultural asset in Mali, but it faces a principal threat. The proliferation of counterfeits and reproductions undermines its history and the expertise that practitioners and advocates like Boubacar pour into their work. We have all seen machine-printed or -sewn designs that mimic mudcloth

LEFT AND BELOW
*Leaves and tree bark
are soaked and boiled.*

LEFT
*Various natural
materials are used,
including the leaves
and bark of the
ngalama tree.*

RIGHT
*Rinsing the textiles is
a two-person job.*

BELOW, LEFT
*Mud clay harvested
from the banks of
the Niger River.*

BELOW, RIGHT
*Soap and shea
butter mixture.*

OPPOSITE
*The entire process is
extremely labor- and
water-intensive, and
Le Ndomo easily uses a
thousand liters a day;
to preserve resources,
Boubacar developed
a natural filtration
system that purifies the
water for reuse.*

in myriad home products and places, described crudely as "tribal" or "African." This gives the home decor industry, and us as consumers, a glaring opportunity to examine our relationship to these decorative objects that are "inspired" by African cultures but do not benefit the people economically nor in recognition. I am an unequivocal advocate for authentic products that promote and center the object's cultural origin as directly as possible. Boubacar makes space for this reciprocity in Le Ndomo's ecosystem. ●

THE AFRICAN DECOR EDIT

KUBA CLOTH, DEMOCRATIC REPUBLIC OF CONGO

ADÈLE BOPE

•

Master of applique Kuba Cloth in Kinshasha

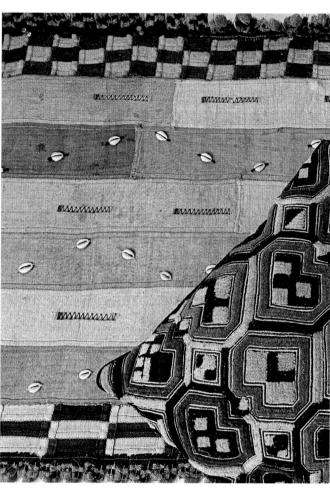

ABOVE
Detail of a flatwoven and quilted Kuba cloth skirt, and a cut-pile pillow cover.

OPPOSITE
Maman Adèle is matriarch of a group of Kuba cloth artisans in Kinshasa.

KUBA CLOTH IS BOTH literally and figuratively a central figure in the evolution of contemporary global home decor. Made exclusively in the Democratic Republic of Congo (DRC), Kuba cloth derives its name from the Bakuba people, who are from the central province of Kasaï. DRC is massive. It is Africa's second largest country by area, and one of the richest in natural and cultural resources. It is also home to the Kuba Kingdom, which flourished during the sixteenth and seventeenth centuries as a highly organized and democratic society.

A tradition that dates back over four hundred years, Kuba cloth's design vernacular has influenced the modernism of Western artists and painters such as Pablo Picasso and Henri Matisse, who openly venerated Kuba cloth. Matisse's studio was full of it, and some surmise that Kuba cloth inspired his 1947 *Les Velours* (The Velvets) paper cut-out series. "I never tire of looking at [the cloth] for long periods of time, even the simplest of them, and waiting for something to come to me from the mystery of their instinctive geometry," he once told British journalist and biographer Hilary Spurling.

One of the guardians of this tradition is Adèle Bope (Maman Adèle). She was born in Mushenge in the Kasaï province, the capital of the Kuba Kingdom. She is part of the Kasaï-Luba tribe, and the making of Kuba cloth is her birthright. She started learning from her grandmother when she was five years old.

She now lives in Nsele township, in Kinshasa's outskirts, over three hundred miles west of Kasaï, where the roads are lined with raffia palm trees. Maman Adèle is considered a mother by the group of

ABOVE
One of Maman Adèle's colleagues prepares the dyed raffia for softening before sewing and threading.

LEFT
The workshop is both a social gathering and workspace for artisans.

LEFT
*Paul Mikombo Bope
is a renowned elder
statesman of the royal
court and advisor to
the king. In this image,
he is wearing tradi-
tional ceremonial Kuba
cloths. He was one of
the original members
of the royal court.*

women she weaves with in Kinshasa, but she is also the mother to eight children, six boys and two girls, all of whom make Kuba cloth. She taught them herself, and she has already started to teach her grandkids.

Kuba cloth was originally reserved for Bakuba kings as their standard regalia during ceremonies. Smaller pieces were used as adornment for the stools and chairs of prominent individuals. The larger pieces (up to twenty feet long) were wrapped several times around the king, a member of the Kuba Court, or a ceremonial performer and worn as a skirt. Women also wore Kuba cloth for up to six months to honor the death of a family member.

BELOW
Artisans compose the designs layer by layer, one fiber at a time.

RIGHT
A panel of embroidered Kuba cloth designed and created by Maman Adèle.

BOTTOM
A quilted and embroidered Kuba cloth skirt on display in my parents' guestroom.

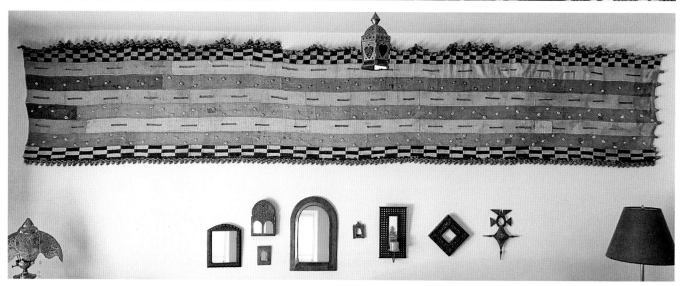

Today, Kuba cloth is seen throughout the facets of Congolese society.

Although its geometry appears random to the untrained eye, Kuba cloth in fact carries symbols that indicate social status or occasion (the more ornate pieces were designed for kings). Some symbols are still only permitted on clothing for royalty, and they can only be worn by a non-royal if prior approval is sought—violators will be fined. Symbols permitted for the general population are mostly those that we find on the home decor of today. One such pattern is the Mikope Ngoma, an interlocking repetition of tufted diamond shapes. Artisans sometimes add pom-pom-like trim (also made from raffia) and cowrie shells to further elevate finished pieces.

Plain-woven raffia, similar to burlap but softer, is the base of each type of cloth. Most Kuba cloth fits into two main categories: appliqué and cut-pile. Adèle cuts and sews each appliqué onto the plain-woven base, creating a dazzling patchwork textile. These panels can then be quilted together to form a skirt in a way that renders seams almost invisible in the pattern's overall constellation. Cut-pile Kuba cloth is thick and coarse, which is why it was traditionally used for seating. Each raffia fiber is sewn through the base, knotted, and cut down to mere millimeters in height. This is repeated hundreds (sometimes thousands) of times, with the artisan's creative and cultural intuitiveness slowly taking a tangible form.

Kuba cloth is still made in much the same way it was in the sixteenth century. Apart from the introduction of artificial dyes (which Maman Adèle says are expensive), everything is the same. Traditional Kuba cloth dyes, and the materials in general, are made from plants within the artisan's immediate environment, but they are less present in heavily urbanized Kinshasa and must be purchased from the market.

The artisans complete similar tasks together, and this is also a time for socializing. As they soften and knead the raffia for the base piece, they form a steady rhythm by singing in unison. The women also create the embroidery thread from raffia in the same manner until it reaches an even finer state. For this, they run the outer lip of a large seashell up and down along the coarse raffia, giving way to a soft and silky texture.

Older pieces are generally more expensive, and price increases with size and the level of ornamentation. Kuba is precious but it is not "perfect," nor is it meant to be, and each set of artisan hands always tells its own story. Any overly simplistic patterns, perfect lines, or literal symmetries are considered inferior, and usually indicate hasty production for the tourist market. But far afield of Adèle's workshops, Kuba cloth's vast mass reproduction in printed forms further threatens this balance. Maman Adèle and her team are happy that their culture is getting this level of exposure, but they want to be sure that their communities benefit economically from its popularization. This has yet to happen.

Maman Adèle's customer profile has also changed with the times (and location). She had a steady flow of customers in Kasaï, who purchased for holidays and special occasions, but the orders were small. However, in Kinshasa, she occasionally has access to larger orders, typically for reselling overseas as opposed to for her direct customer's personal use. Priests and missionaries were the regulars in town, but overall demand has decreased due to her lack of access to buyers who have shifted to e-commerce and social media—and counterfeits.

It is hard to imagine that artisans like Maman Adèle are facing a decreased demand for their work. Kuba cloth is, and has been, an African and modern decor standard for decades. To what degree artisans like Adèle benefit from their culture-turned-commerce enough to thrive economically depends on factors outside of their control. But her precise reasons for continuing her work are the heart of the matter: "I am proud of my culture and repeating what my grandmother was doing." I would love to see Kuba cloth persist in an impactful and honorable way for centuries more to come. ●

04

WALLS AND FLOORS

PERHAPS ONE OF THE most established ways to incorporate African decor into your home is with wall decor and rugs. African artisans have long created exquisite rugs and handcrafts brimming with cultural significance, and each has emerged as a keystone of African-inspired interiors. The pieces and artisans in this section offer unique stories: From Catherine and Abdoulaye in Western Cameroon to Naima in Morocco's Atlas Mountains, all represent a persisting element of their respective cultural heritage. Experience the beauty of their work and communities as we head to places off the beaten path.

LEFT
Finished rugs hang to dry.

THE AFRICAN DECOR EDIT

MOROCCAN RUGS, MOROCCO

NAIMA ABEKAN

Weaver and founder of Cooperative Fadel Tighedouine, Tighedouine

ABOVE
Naima and her artisans in front of their loom.

TOP
Four weavers at the loom.

OPPOSITE
Naima Abekan, Founder and President of Cooperative Fadel in her hometown of Tighedouine, Morocco.

THE DAY STARTED OUT with a cool breeze in the air, a stark departure from the dense streets and instant heat of June in Marrakech. The day's visit was to Tighedouine in the Atlas Mountains, a drive of about an hour and thirty minutes from Marrakech. The central artery consists of little more than one road in and one road out, but it's a bustling road. About one mile in and up a rocky overlook to the left is where you will find the home of Naima peering down on the busy day below, with a view of the rust-colored mountains across the valley.

Naima's home also houses Fadel Tighedouine, the rug weaving cooperative she founded in 1999. The outside of the cooperative is deceptively nondescript and betrays little of the beauty inside. It almost disappears into the landscape as if it were one with the mountain. Naima was born in this home.

Stepping inside, I am greeted by hurried hands on an imposing loom called a *mensej* in Arabic. Four women are at the helm, surrounded by a gaggle of children. Most of the artisan workspaces I visit integrate various aspects of life, and small children are usually present. The artisans remain focused on the task at hand, and the act of childcare is a communal one, made easier because there are several mothers and children of different ages to make sure the children are looked after so the day's work gets done. Approximately thirty women belong to Naima's cooperative, mostly coming from the same village. The workday typically runs from ten thirty in the morning to five in the late afternoon, and the more complex designs call for more women.

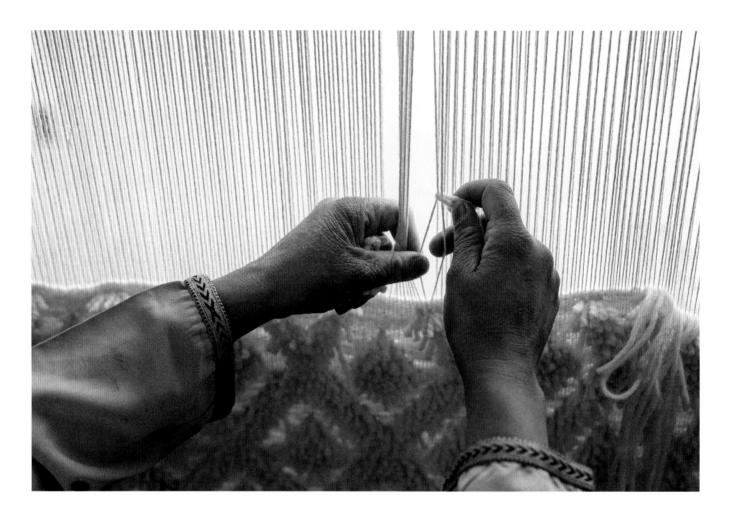

It goes without saying that these rugs are an interior design classic, but rug weaving in Morocco is a sacred tradition. Naima's work in the trade began when she was twelve years old, when she learned how to weave from her mother. Initially, she embroidered small designs into handkerchiefs and napkins, mainly as a hobby. Soon after, her mother became ill and the domestic responsibilities fell to Naima. Over time, she became the local authority on rug weaving.

Still, entrepreneurship is not for the faint of heart, and Naima has experienced her own set of challenges as an independent artisan and cooperative president. Because of Tighedouine's relatively isolated location from Marrakech (the main tourism and commercial center of the region), poor roads and the cost of transportation mean that she can't always reach reliable sales channels. These conditions also restrict access to quality materials and supplies. And sometimes the group members do not get along, which can slow down the work.

Five years ago, Naima partnered with an umbrella cooperative with a mission to create an artisan-owned and -managed craft economy. The umbrella cooperative works with a network of independent cooperatives throughout Morocco to provide quality control, training, materials, and other operational services to its members. Color-coded wool samples are one way in which Naima's work has been standardized as a result of this partnership, so she knows exactly what color—and quality—wool she will receive. This part of the process deviates significantly from the traditional manner of artisans completing all the work themselves. Those steps include gathering plants for natural dyes (such as olives, chamomile flowers, and henna leaves), brushing, and spinning wool.

LEFT
A rug can contain over 50,000 knots.

BELOW
The tasgah *on the right is used for pounding each knot into place.*

OPPOSITE
Knotting styles are sometimes specific to particular families and lineages.

LEFT
A sample of one of Naima's cooperative's flatwoven kilim rugs.

OPPOSITE
The wooden jepet *can span several meters and controls the size of the rug on the loom.*

LEFT
Naima receives the coded wool samples from her umbrella organization.

During our visit, Naima's women were working on a bulk rug order. Naima's group was responsible for seven rugs, while the remainder of the order was split across the other cooperatives in the network. The rug on the loom measured about three by four meters; they had already been working on it for ten days, and they still had a week to go before it was finished.

This group specializes in a variety of traditional styles, which are primarily the plush low-to-high pile rugs, flatwoven kilim and Zanafi rugs, and Boucherouite rugs made of repurposed and recycled materials. They all come from different regions. For example, the flatwoven kilim rugs originate among the villages of southeastern Morocco. The more plush Beni Ourain style is common in the mid-Atlas Mountain regions, where Naima is based. All Moroccan rugs are said to have protective powers. This starts with the loom that each is made on, which is also said to possess magical attributes.

Naima has big dreams for her cooperative. With the steady influx of orders she receives from the partnership, she can focus on investments in growing her workspace and home. Shortly before our visit, the structure where she lives and works was damaged by a severe windstorm—fortunately nobody was hurt. Rather than adding to the existing structure beyond the repairs, she would like to begin anew by creating a separate place to work altogether.

Beyond providing Naima with a comfortable life, this work has been a refuge for her during some of the most difficult times. Though she lost both of her parents and dropped out of school when she was still young, weaving has been a consistent outlet for her to express both her creativity and cultural pride. She is an anchor for the women in her community and beyond, and spaces such as Naima's are a vital part of Moroccan culture and its economy. ●

JUJU HATS, CAMEROON

CATHERINE LONTSE

•

Weaver of Bafoussam

OPPOSITE
Catherine greets us in her boutique where she works and sells her Juju hats.

ABOVE
These feathers are tightly tied around wooden slats and ready to be woven to the raffia base, one at a time.

ABOVE
Catherine was making this Juju hat during my visit.

CATHERINE'S BOUTIQUE IN BAFOUSSAM, Cameroon, is not the kind of place that you happen upon. Located deep inside of a winding craft and clothing market with tight aisles, you won't find her without a guide or a keen sense of direction. Catherine calls the six-foot-by-six-foot stall that she works and sells out of her "boutique." When the wares that you make and sell are as regal as these, it's not difficult to make such a compact space feel grand. Juju hats, also known as Tyn hats in Cameroon, are her specialty, and they line the walls of the boutique's three sides from floor to ceiling. There is exactly one Bamileke stool, which she offers me during my visit, and one chair, which she works from at the edge of the space. From there, she can more easily chat with her neighbors and passersby. It's all rather efficient.

Catherine has been making Juju hats for ten years. She had an unconventional journey into the specialty. She was a market woman selling fish for most of her adult life until she experienced an illness that prevented her from being able to work in that capacity for many months. As a mother of eight children, she still needed to be able to bring in household income, and she was approached by a man her son knew to help with his Juju hat business. Because she used to embroider on clothing and accessories as a hobby, she took to the craft quickly, and decided to continue with it once she made a full recovery. The same man who brought her on to help him then trained her so that she could start her own business.

Juju hats are symbols of honors, elegance, and distinction; in the Western Grasslands region of

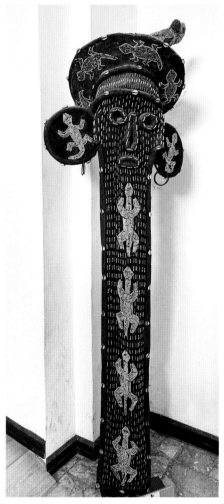

RIGHT
The Mbap Mteng at the Musée National du Cameroun stands almost seven feet tall. A juju hat sits atop this mask, with the feathers facing upward toward the sky.

Cameroon, the Bamileke people still use them for traditional ceremonies. They are worn by advisors to the king, or the *fon* as the king is called in the Bamileke language, and also during a chief's burial. These days, Juju hats are also worn during more secular events such as birthdays and anniversaries. I did not see them used as decoration in any portion of the country during my time in Cameroon.

Catherine sells mainly to local customers for ceremonies and to tourists, and she helps other artisans who receive large orders by sharing the workload (a common practice among many of the weavers). Each hat takes two to three days to make, and sizes range from eighteen to more than thirty inches in diameter. In the traditional context, the bigger the hat, the more important the wearer. When not in use, Juju hats are folded neatly into a cylindrical shape, and they only weigh three pounds at most.

The materials and manner of making the Juju hats has not changed much since Catherine started in this line of work. She still uses fowl feathers, lightweight wooden slats, raffia for the base, and twine (or sometimes plastic string). The most drastic changes are the

Juju hats fold into a lightweight and compact cylinder shape. An Ndop textile is in the background.

LEFT
Catherine's boutique is just off a bustling artery within a winding marketplace.

BELOW
Catherine sources a variety of feathers from the other side of the market where she works. The feathers come from chickens, ducks, and sometimes turkeys.

LEFT
Powdered dyes are formulated specifically for the feathers used in this process.

OPPOSITE
This duck-feathered Juju hat came home with me!

vibrant colors that Juju can be found in today as a result of imported and artificial dyes, which Catherine buys from her neighbor in the market. Colors were traditionally dictated by the types of birds found in Bafoussam and skewed more neutral. Colorful varieties were available but rare due to the difficult nature of acquiring the feathers. Bright greens, for example, came from parrots. Since African societies do not tend to kill or harm animals for the singular purpose of design and adornment, neutral colors were the most common.

Beyond sharing the workload, there's another interesting way in which Juju hat artisans support one another. It is common for female entrepreneurs in Cameroon to finance their businesses through a long-standing communal system called "buy am, sell am" or Njdangui. Each woman contributes a small amount per week (or another frequency), and each week one woman receives the lump sum. There are different levels and different amounts, and the recipient is selected based on seniority, by lottery, or by request. Certain groups now also include prizes such as appliances, purses, and wigs. This self-governing finance model predates modern banking in Cameroon, and it remains the most accessible for rural women seeking to establish a foothold for building their local businesses.

Catherine has made a comfortable life for herself, and she is able to handle all her main costs of living. She thinks that this line of work could be even more profitable if certain conditions would improve. Sophisticated Indigenous systems and timeworn relationships afford entrepreneurial artisans a versatile system of support, and this trend has proven beneficial for Catherine throughout her career. There's a mutual dependence and reciprocity within these networks, the advantages of which emanate throughout their society for a common good. Such artisanal cottage industries in Cameroon are part and parcel of an ecosystem that nourishes livelihoods like Catherine's, and in turn, the country as a whole. ◉

THE AFRICAN DECOR EDIT

BAMUM SHIELDS, CAMEROON

ABDOULAYE MEFIRE

Woodcarver of Manka

OPPOSITE
Abdoulaye is adept at carving the shields that his ethnic group is known for. He has also learned how to carve the tall Bwa mask from Burkina Faso.

ABOVE
Abdoulaye's goods are sold in markets such as this one in Marrakech.

ABDOULAYE'S OPEN AIR STUDIO is perched atop a modest hill in the residential neighborhood of Manka in Foumban. By the time I reached his studio in the late afternoon, school was letting out and children were beginning to congregate in this social hub. It became evident to me, yet again, that artisan workspaces serve a social and communal function. They are informal gathering spots for multiple generations to discuss the events of the day or the news of the moment.

This father of four is an expert woodcarver whose specialty is Bamum shields. Popularly known as Bamileke shields, Bamum shields originate in Cameroon's Western Grassland region. More precisely, they're made in Foumban, an ancient kingdom that was once ruled by two brothers and eventually split along those lines. Bamum people created their own language and customs, and they would become the custodians of this woodcarving tradition.

Abdoulaye's modest atelier, which he started over twenty years ago, doesn't indicate the international scope of his enterprise. While he produces the Bamum shields and trains other young men in the skillset, his brothers living in other parts of Africa sell his work. Countries like Senegal, Morocco, and South Africa have well-developed tourist markets in comparison to Cameroon, and the demand is there. In what is effectively a family enterprise, Abdoulaye's brothers have established shops and contacts in Africa's key tourist destinations to sell his work. Like his brothers, Abdoulaye started his business with his own savings. But *unlike* them, woodcarving has been Abdoulaye's lifelong passion, and despite having opportunities to join his brothers abroad, he chooses his craft every day. His Bamum

ABOVE
Abdoulaye's studio is also an informal community gathering place.

RIGHT
Jamaal is Abdoulaye's nephew, whom he is currently teaching the art of shield making.

shield–making business can truly be done only in Cameroon, for ecological reasons.

Beyond the reasons that Mother Nature dictates, Bamum shields originated here due to their cultural significance. Abdoulaye tells me that like all shields, they were used during bouts of war and conflicts between ethnic groups. But what distinguishes them from other wartime accouterments are their carved, highly symmetrical designs. This element is characteristic of these shields and was designed to create visual confusion for the enemies. You can imagine seeing tens or even hundreds of these shields lined up and trying to strategize any plan of attack—it must have been confusing indeed! Bamum shields are made from the iconic and ancient baobab tree, found primarily throughout Africa's semi-arid and dry climates. Abdoulaye sources the baobab from neighboring regions, sometimes up to fifty kilometers away, where the forests are thicker. But he can't just go and cut down a tree. He has had long standing relationships with various village chiefs, and he must first get their permission and negotiate a price. Once the formalities are settled, it can take up to a week for Abdoulaye to cut the baobab down to size. He cuts the tree down into wood panels measuring

ABOVE
The tools of the trade have remained the same over the years. Machines are never involved.

RIGHT
Artisans draw very precise and geometric designs on the shield using pencil and chalk.

LEFT
Cameroon's baobab
trees are ubiquitous in
this western part of the
country.

up to 24 inches square by 3 inches, and each shield is made from one of these pieces. He shows me a grainy video on his smartphone from the site and it is no doubt laborious. Baobab is his tree of choice because its timber is durable yet soft relative to other trees found in Cameroon and is therefore easy to carve.

Once Abdoulaye is back at his atelier, the work begins, and the entire process takes at least one day per shield. The panels are first put out in the sun to dry, and depending on the size of order, he can assign up to ten boys and men to work with him. During my visit, there were two men (including Abdoulaye) and one apprentice making shields. Their instruments have not changed much over time, and I was genuinely impressed by their ability to make such precisely round shapes with only a machete. Even the rounding on the edges is achieved with this tool, and the finer carvings are then made with a *petit scissors*. Machines are not used during any stage of the design process, not even man-powered ones. The artisan chips away at the squared edges whilst turning it, forming a fluid rhythm that gradually reveals

a perfectly circular shape. Depending on the level of concretion and the final form, the shaving and carving can take several hours per shield.

Once the perfectly rounded shields are cut, pencil drawings begin to give way to the imminent carvings. The drawings are always perfectly symmetrical, and a pencil tethered to the center of the shield aids in this precision. The next step is what gives the shields their mildly smoky aroma, which lingers as a reminder of its origins even after many months. Upwards of thirty shields can be placed in an outdoor fire pit where they are scorched and charred for about half a day, giving each shield its permanent blackish-brown appearance. From that point, the artisan carefully adds a locally sourced mineral clay mixture, known locally as *kalaba*, into each groove, giving the shield its final duochromatic appearance.

When asked what inspires him to continue on the artisan side, rather than the more financially lucrative path of his brothers, Abdoulaye tells me, "I have tried other activities, but this is in my blood." •

ABOVE
Baobab planks dry in the sun before carving begins.

LEFT
Abdoulaye must be swift and certain as he creates each shield's circular shape from the original rectangular boards.

AFRICAN DECOR AT HOME

05

HERE IS YOUR PASSPORT for a journey to visit ten innovative and impeccably styled homes in locations around the world. Each home has its own distinctive character and story, and all are also united by the central theme of African decor. From New York to Los Angeles, London to Berlin, these creative homeowners offer their perspectives on what it means to design, decorate, and live with African decor. Two residences in Africa are also included, to explore the significance of decorating with African objects when you are already there. Here is African-inspired decorating at its finest.

YOU
ARE
MAGIC

African Style

Margaret Courtney-Clarke
Foreword by Maya Angelou

AN CANVAS

MANDELA

OPPOSITE
I define my personal style as African-Modern—and sometimes vintage.

ABOVE
My home is a seventies open concept, so I create different zones with rugs and seating arrangements.

Decidedly African Modern
Nasozi Kakembo

MARYLAND, USA

THE AFRICAN DECOR EDIT

MY **1800**S BROOKLYN BROWNSTONE
(and first apartment) was replete with original details,
such as original shutters and millwork; for eight years
it was my lab and the focus of my design experiments,
allowing me to explore with my evolving interior preferences. That apartment cemented my design style.

My current home, a townhome in Maryland, is the
epitome of an entirely different era—1970s contemporary.
Typical of the time, it has little non-utilitarian ornament.
That allows me to embrace the architectural design elements (like vaulted ceilings) and a nontraditional layout
instead (my bedroom is downstairs, and my office is
a loft overlooking the living room). The space possesses
a distinct character that I have personalized with the
texture, dimension, and warmth of African decor.

LEFT
*I have a lot of coffee
table books and no
coffee table—the perfect
excuse for having a
collection of African
stools instead!*

———

TIP
Bolga baskets
from Ghana are
multipurpose:
I use them as
sculpture—and
for storing
firewood. **V**

My decor is decidedly African and African-inspired. I've flirted with other design looks, only to find my way back to this seminal style.

TIP

Use Kuba cloth tapestry, such as this flatwoven appliqued piece, to highlight an area—as above the console here.

BELOW
This Cesca chair was reupholstered in various bogolan fabrics, including a vintage bogolan from my mom.

I cherish my home, and every time I introduce a new object that expands my understanding of African history and culture, it gets even better.

My decor is decidedly African and African-inspired. I've flirted with other design looks, only to find my way back to this seminal style. African aesthetics also go well in many design schemes: I love mixing in vintage and classic details.

I rarely introduce reproductions into my decor scheme. It's partially a matter of principle, and I've saved up for months and sometimes years in some cases to be able to invest in authentic items. I'm currently saving for a Senufo bed!

My favorite online destination for sourcing home goods is my own xN Studio (because I always get first picks). Marrakech is another favorite destination for sourcing: There's nothing from the African continent you can't find there. I also like shopping in Accra for similar reasons. Locally (and by locally I mostly mean Brooklyn), I love Peace & Riot and Lamine at the Brooklyn Flea. I also found a cool spot in Berlin called Annie's African Art in Schöneberg that is owned and operated by a German woman of Kenyan descent.

If you are seeking to incorporate more African-made home goods into your space, I would offer this advice:

African decor is as utilitarian as it is beautiful, so switching out a mass-produced or uninspiring item for a handcrafted African one is an easy way to start. Baskets are an accessible gateway, and you can never have enough. I have a stockpile of wares in my personal collection, and I curate them depending on the season and my mood. You don't have to use or showcase all of your decorative objects at once, or even keep them in the same room forever. Most of my pieces have occupied at least two rooms in my home. This is one way to keep your rooms and your objects feeling like new.

—————
TIP
Style a bookcase or shelf
with items of a similar
height to create visual
harmony and variety.
Here, I paired a miniature
Ndop stool from Nigeria
with woodcarvings from
Uganda.

<

OPPOSITE
Open kitchen shelving lets me have fun with this batik-inspired wallpaper.

RIGHT
Vintage indigo textiles from Mali are extremely absorbent. Use them in a powder room as a hand towel for practical whimsy. The peel-and-stick wallpaper mimics the same dyeing technique to a T.

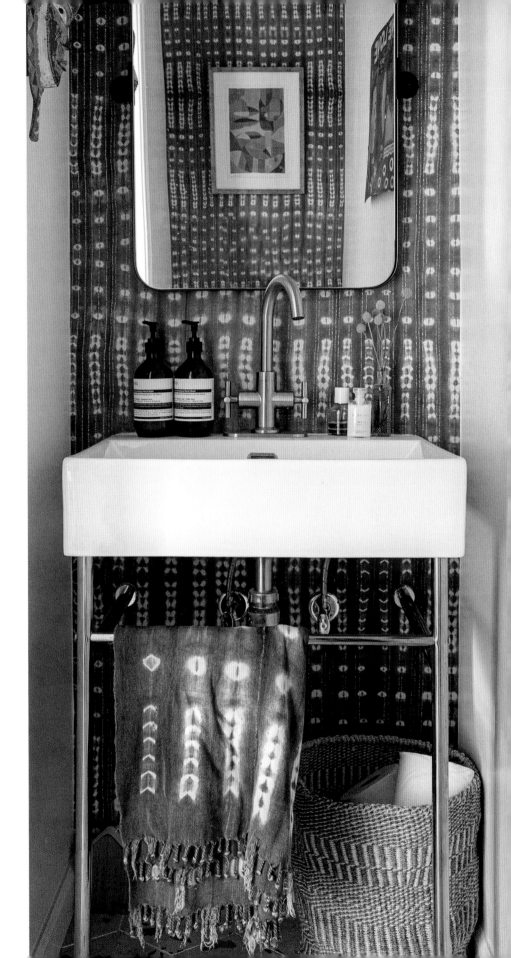

THE AFRICAN DECOR EDIT

LEFT
*Never feel obligated
to match pillows and
textiles: Their organic
nature pulls them all
together.*

Right now, my favorite pieces are my pillows. They were the only product I sold when I started my company, and I have over a decade's worth of samples as well as newer designs that I experiment with constantly. I switch out my pillow covers every season or even more often, and it's just so fun! It keeps my home feeling fresh.

Some of the pieces I've collected remind me of when I first started my business. The prototype for my mudcloth bench is still at the dining room table, albeit in tatters. I made it from the mudcloth my mother sent with me to Brooklyn in 2005—I simply can't part with it. The ebibbo are a constant reminder of Uganda, my family there, and the sacrifices that both of my parents made at various points in their lives.

As with all collections, there are many special memories in mine; the foundational pieces are the ones my mother gifted me, including the aforementioned mudcloth, a Korhogo cloth painting, and a Bolga basket that she got during a trip to Ghana.

OPPOSITE
Play up ceiling angles and height with bold accents like this Korhogo cloth.

ABOVE AND RIGHT
The cobweb design of the Bamum stool in my primary bathroom represents wisdom. The raffia wall plates are from Uganda.

I think about the African home goods industry a lot. African home decor and the communities they come from have every reason to thrive, and I would love to see more African artisans benefiting directly from their work. I would also love to see an end to the small-scale and mass production of counterfeit African decor, and for the market demand for those items to be met with authentic goods made in Africa, within the communities where the objects originate. ●

City Mews Oasis
Hana Getachew

LONDON, UNITED KINGDOM

OPPOSITE
Hana Getachew is the founder and creative director of Bolé Road Textiles. We visited her artisans in the Textiles section (see page 77).

ABOVE
Accent pillows are one of the easiest ways to personalize a space with African decor. Here, Hana coordinates them with the bold colors in the already-furnished living room.

HANA GETACHEW'S LONDON HOME is a master class in how to turn temporary accommodations—a rental, home away from home, or otherwise—into an oasis for a family of three. Although home base is still New York, Hana, her husband, and her young daughter left their longtime Brooklyn apartment (and weekend home upstate) for a one-year stint in London. Even though their Chelsea accommodations would only be theirs for twelve months, making the partially furnished rental feel like their own was a top priority.

Hana is an interior designer with her own signature line of home goods, so she has both the inspiration and collected accents to make her home-away-from-home feel anything but fleeting. Using her ever-expanding line of home textiles, which she partners with artisans in Ethiopia (see page 77) to create, Hana has transformed an otherwise standard long-term rental into a timeless space filled with personal design.

The Chelsea neighborhood where Hana lives has rows of charming and pristine white mews and blooming window boxes. (Mews are former horse stables, now converted into homes, and they're quite common in parts of central London.)

In terms of style, Hana aspires to be a minimalist but admits, "I have home envy whenever I'm in a maximalist space!" She ends up somewhere in between, employing a simple backdrop that she makes interesting by adding a range of textures.

Hana defines this type of backdrop as having "a good layout, natural light, and nice architectural details, which I think our London home has." From there, she slowly layers in furniture, accessories, and art.

Since she is always incorporating African accents in her homes, her advice comes from experience: "If you want to incorporate more African-made home goods into your space, my number one tip would be to look for authentic pieces sold by African artisans,

ABOVE
Each of Hana's pillows is handwoven by artisan partners in Ethiopia.

ABOVE
Bright colors coordinate with neutral pillows in the secondary living room.

TIP Λ

Small flatwoven rugs add warmth, both visually and practically. Since many African textiles are super-absorbent, due to the high quality of cotton used to make them, they make great towels (and bathrobes). **>**

designers, or resellers. Living in NYC and London is wonderful for this since there are so many market-places and pop-ups." For those not living in a bustling urban metropolis, Hana points to resources online: "It just takes a bit of research." When she moved into her first apartment in Harlem, she purchased some wax print African fabrics from the Malcolm Shabazz Harlem Market on 116th and Lennox to decorate with. (This market is an excellent and historic source for African fabrics and goods in New York City.) From there, she wrapped the textiles on canvases and placed them along her walls as artwork.

My number one tip would be to look for authentic pieces sold by African artisans, designers, or resellers.

That was long before she started her own line of textile-based home decor, which she of course now favors. Since London is a temporary stay, Hana and her family chose to travel light, bringing favorite tex-tiles, instead of lots of furniture and decor, from home in New York. This included table linens, pillow covers, and throws (accumulated over the years through Hana's business). These provided a sense of familiarity and comfort in their new home, far from Brooklyn.

ABOVE
A simple tea towel adds color at the kitchen sink.

LEFT
Table runners are another easy way to incorporate flatwoven African textiles into your decor scheme.

The textiles not only remind Hana of Brooklyn, but of Ethiopia as well. In fact, she started her business to be more connected to the place where she was born. Having Ethiopian-made textiles all around her home is a part of that. "It also is something I can share with my daughter. I can teach her about the traditions and heritage of our country through the pieces in our home."

While in London, Hana launched a collaboration with a major national home decor retailer. (It was the largest order that she and her artisans had ever worked on together.) During the production process she collected a few samples, but after the launch she ended up redecorating her entire home with pieces from the new collaboration. "Even though we only have a few months left to live here," she laughs, "it was worth the effort!"

ABOVE
A snapshot of the design process.

LEFT
Hana's home office.

LEFT
Large baskets, such as this one from Ethiopia, are perfect decorative storage for toys.

———

TIP
Pillows aren't just for the indoors! Add bright tactile accents to create a defined outdoor oasis. >

As a proud designer from the African diaspora, Hana is committed to creating a bridge between her clients and the talented artisans of Africa. "I would love to see the African home goods and handmade industry grow and thrive," says Hana. "There is such richness in materials, skills, and history in so many craft traditions within the continent; it would be wonderful for these communities to gain more recognition." There is certainly a market for well-made, sustainable, authentic products. ●

Island Sanctuary
Nina Farmer

MARTHA'S VINEYARD, MASSACHUSETTS, USA

ABOVE
*Nina's home is situated steps
away from Lambert's Cove Beach;
surfboards are at the ready.*

OPPOSITE
The Farmer family of four.

MARTHA'S VINEYARD is a sanctuary island.
Long before it made headlines for being a summer
destination for US presidents, it was home to the
Wampanoag Native Americans, who still reside there
today. *Noepe* is the island's original, Indigenous name,
and the island remains accessible only by ferry and
plane (weather permitting).

Boston-based interior designer Nina Farmer and
her family have made Martha's Vineyard their summer haven for a generation. Since my own family on
my mother's side has been on the island for over four
decades, Nina's home is a truly special one for me to
share in these pages.

Located just off Lambert's Cove Beach, Nina's idyllic
refuge for her family of four blends the casual Vineyard
aesthetic with elements from her travels and artistic
interests. Working mostly with classical New England
design elements and old-world European references,
Nina infuses timelessness into all her projects—including her own home. Here, she gets to kick her shoes off,
so to speak, and to explore a personal kind of tradition
and aesthetic for her family's rustic summer retreat.

TIP
Stools are not just for seating.
A traditional Bamum stool
can double as a side table. **>**

The house itself is in West Tisbury, one of five small towns on the island. It's an "up-island" town, which is a local term for the more secluded enclaves. Up-island is more rural than Vineyard Haven and Oak Bluffs, which both have areas with more of a downtown feeling where the ferries dock.

Nina's style is steeped in the classics, with a global perspective: Travel has been a huge influence, and she loves incorporating colors, textures, and materials from all over the world. "I have always been drawn to African accents," she confesses. "When I moved into my first home my mother gifted me a pair of Benin Bronze Oba heads, which I cherish. Over time, I have added various African sculptures to my collection, and was most recently inspired by a family trip to the Masai region in Kenya."

"Morocco is my favorite destination for sourcing African home goods. There is a significant value placed on handicrafts and decorative elements such as textiles and tile. There are also so many influences infused in the objects and the assortment in the souks."

When asked what tips she would offer to incorporate more African-made home goods into a space, she replies, "I would start by looking for an African rug, and of course Morocco has an endless assortment. I always select the rug first because it anchors a space and gives you a good starting point to build from."

"Favorite pieces that I absolutely adore are the Ethiopian carved chair that's in the kitchen. I also cherish all the Moroccan pottery pieces that I brought home from my travels. And of course the Benin bronzes were among my favorites from my very first home."

LEFT
A single bold item, like this bedspread from Morocco, can transform a small room.

PREVIOUS SPREAD
*Open shelving isn't just for dishes.
Nina adds textural contrast with
conical Rwandan Agaseke baskets.
Traditionally, these hold beans and
rice following a wedding.*

RIGHT
*A Fang mask from Gabon accen-
tuates the kitchen's whitewashed
palette. Conical Rwandan Agaseke
baskets (traditionally used to hold
beans and rice following a wedding) are practical and decorative
on open shelves.*

Each item conveys special meaning, both to Nina and her family.

Because of the plethora of untapped
talent that is available, she would love
to see more artists' work from African
countries spotlighted. "I have tried to
share the joys of travel with my girls
and pass along the idea that the world is
large and worth exploring. Both of them
have studied Africa extensively and are
very proud that they can name and
identify every country, capital, and flag.
Being surrounded by beautifully crafted
items from across the globe helps to
feel connected."

LEFT
Indigo pillows from Mali and golden leather Moroccan poufs invite comfort and camaraderie in the den.

————

TIP
Mudcloth accent pillows add texture and interest.

V

Each item conveys special meaning, both to Nina and her family. "Some of the pieces have been acquired through my own travels and some I have inherited. I have two ebony carved busts from West Africa (modern-day Liberia) that my husband's grandfather picked up when he flew for Pan American airlines. I have a romantic idea of what travel looked like in the 1940s before globalization took hold, and these pieces connect us to certain times in history." ●

A Space Designed for *Artist Renée C. Neblett*

KOKROBITE, GHANA

OPPOSITE
Renée looks out onto Kokrobitey's lush canopy.

LEFT
All of Kokrobitey's buildings are plastered with laterite, a sustainable local material that the late architect (and dear friend to Renée) Alero Olympio championed in her work.

RENÉE C. NEBLETT, known affectionately in the Greater Accra region as "Aunty Renée," is the consummate multi-hyphenate— a poet and writer, a visual artist, a Boston native, and a former Harvard Bunting fellow, just for starters. She spent years in Dusseldorf before relocating to Ghana. I first visited her home (and life's work) when I came for a batik textile residency at her renowned research and development facility, the Kokrobitey Institute. The sustainability-focused Institute, and its Alero Olympio Design Center, were designed by Renée's dear friend the late architect Alero Olympio, and both nod to the pristine land and ways of life found in Kokrobite several decades ago.

Kokrobite is a place between and betwixt traditional Ghanaian culture and the invasion of an emerging market economy. While it's not as verdant and pure as it was when Renée arrived in the late 1980s, it still has not been completely eroded. Back then, Kokrobite was a virtual paradise—a pristine fishing village whose streets were lined with bungalows and shaded by mature trees of all kinds.

TIP

A Senufo bed makes for a stately coffee table if you can get your hands on one (they are mostly sold in galleries and at auction houses outside of Western Africa).

LEFT
Renée adheres to clean lines and minimalist furniture in her private residence; textiles from northern Ghana cover the integrated bench seating.

————

TIP
Mix, don't match! Embrace different furniture styles that still complement one another, such as the Senufo and custom side tables.

>

The current decor, created by Renée, is understated and pushes against modern consumerism: She combines traditional forms with discarded reusable materials to create something new. "My key decor principle," she says, "which applies to my design principles more broadly for Kokrobitey's philosophy, is that we must acknowledge tradition and its various forms as the basis of what we do today. My aesthetic is governed by simple lines and natural materials, with a Bauhaus sensibility. I also appropriate waste materials and reinvent them as useful materials for design."

It is important, she feels, to preserve an African aesthetic rather than a mass-produced, imported one. "The world should not be governed by one cultural perspective if we want to sustain ourselves and see ourselves prosper, and traditional knowledge systems have had a huge impact on the world. Once there is a deep critical self-awareness, African countries will recognize that they come from a place of worth, and that what we already have is valuable.

"It often takes an extended period of time of peace and prosperity to be able to self-reflect, and acknowledge who you are, and better articulate to the world what you have. Africa is on the precipice of this Renaissance."

As for her own personal favorite goods, she notes, "I have been collecting traditional African objects, art, and decor for over forty years. Some are from local craftspeople here in Ghana, and others are imported from across the West African region. I bought a 4-wheel-drive SUV for my sixtieth birthday and drove from Ghana to Mali and back. The trip lasted three weeks and I bought some fantastic pieces during that trip, like many of the Dogon doors you see throughout the campus facilities and residences, and my private residence in Accra.

ABOVE

Art for art's sake: Sculptural Bolga baskets can be used simply as decorative statement pieces.

LEFT

Rooms are decorated with treasures from travel and wares from local markets; a Dogon door and Dogon ladder from Mali; Kuba cloth pillows from Congo; and an Ewe bedspread from southeastern Ghana.

Most of what we consider modern has been influenced by the basic forms of traditional African objects

——

"I love some of the Malian woven textiles—all the woven and natural materials. Most forms across Africa are clean and intriguing, but most importantly, they tell a history that is infused with so much meaning."

Renée offers encouragement to would-be collectors who admire her aesthetic. "It starts with your own sense of what is aesthetically pleasing. One must be open to looking, exploring, and ultimately acknowledging the beauty of these authentic pieces. None of these were originally spectator items. Most of what we consider modern has been influenced by the basic forms of traditional African objects, and these forms are a landscape of opportunity."

TIP
Senufo stools come in various sizes and make perfect occasional tables. Try adding a flat surface, such as a tray or book, since the tops are carved with a depression for sitting. ∧

RIGHT
Adongo, the Bolga weaver featured on pages 50–55, made this custom light fixture.

Looking to the future, she notes, "I would love to see African artisans maintain the integrity of their craftsmanship yet be open to appropriating some of these skills and forms in the constitution of new objects and disciplines. In terms of 'how to scale,' they can go back to small, decentralized production units that allow people to work in their own communities whilst fostering intercultural discourse." ●

TIP
Store and style bathroom
linens and accessories in a
multipurpose Bolga market
basket. **∨**

A Flat at the Crossroads
Emma Wingfield

LONDON, UNITED
KINGDOM

THE AFRICAN DECOR EDIT

TIP
Use a small Moroccan rug to anchor a living room without completely covering gorgeous wooden floors. **V**

I MET EMMA at a trade show in New York City, many years after I fell in love with her brand. A textile arts researcher teaching design, culture, and enterprise at the university level in London, Emma attributes her entry into the world of textiles and craftsmanship to a singular event:

She started working with a group of weavers almost a decade ago and has formed lasting relationships—both personal and professional—with the weavers since then. She was usually procuring for clients and customers abroad, but one day, she finally purchased something for herself: an artisanal bedspread, which set the decor direction of her home, and even her field of study. When speaking about that moment, Emma says, "I owe everything I do today to that purchase and the partnership it inspired."

Working with weavers steered her toward an interest in the design of her home space and paying more attention to how things are made, their materials, and the artisan. Through her work in Côte d'Ivoire, she's met numerous artisans and designers, and they've all made items that she now has in her home. Her secondary design principle stems from the townhome's modest footprint—it is compact, so organization is key. And much like the home that they're in, the compact African accents they use for organization and decor have a small footprint but leave a lasting impression. Emma and her husband (and cat, Jemima) live in a relaxed residential neighborhood with lots of pubs, restaurants, and local shops.

OPPOSITE
*Emma's guest bedroom pairs artisan
textiles from Mali and Cote d'Ivoire.*

TIP
A ladder is a visually appealing and practical way to
store textiles when they're
not in use.

>

She describes her husband as a minimalist and herself as "an enemy of clutter," but they both love color and texture. "We tend to gravitate towards a design aesthetic that celebrates individual pieces with natural/grounded colors and tones that bring them all together. Dark greens, dusty yellows, deep blues, and warming browns in natural materials like cotton and wood are our staples for sure. We're also very lucky to know some very talented artists whose work we've started collecting.

"I started decorating with African accents when I was working with a group of weavers in Northern Côte d'Ivoire. I loved the texture of their handwoven cloth and their muted colors.

"Although I am biased toward Côte d'Ivoire, I think there are great things to be found wherever you go. My husband and I went to Morocco for our honeymoon and we bought some water glasses that we use daily. I've hand-carried ceramics/wooden furniture back from all sorts of places, and I love a good browse through antique emporiums. I also love purchasing home goods from friends who have similar companies."

OPPOSITE

*A small Senufo stool is left raw,
in keeping with Emma's natural
wood-colored palette.*

———————

TIP

A discreet, rounded Bolga
basket—used as a planter—
brings warmth to stairwells
or other bare corners.

∨

"Although I am biased toward Côte d'Ivoire, I think there are great things to be found wherever you go."

——

"I started decorating with African accents when I was working with a group of weavers in Northern Côte d'Ivoire. I loved the texture of their handwoven cloth and their muted colors."

———

When shopping for African-made home goods, Emma advises, "Avoid large online marketplaces. I know it is easy to just go to one website to find a bunch of items from different stores, but it is even better when you can order directly from the shop or buy from contemporary artisans/makers/craftspeople. To construct pieces by hand is an art. When thinking about which items to buy, I've found it helps to stick to a color scheme that you love. That will help create an affinity across the objects you curate. For example, the pattern on my artisanal bedspread (one of the first textiles I purchased for myself from the weavers I work with) has inspired not only the design within my home but also my research interest.

"I would love to see a more equal market for craftspeople/artisans across the continent. There are still a lot of barriers that keep the seamless sale of home goods made on the continent from circulating through the global marketplace. There is a difference between sourcing from artisans/craftspeople and actually working with artisans/craftspeople. They are designers and really brilliant at it. I hope in the future more attention is paid to that rather than artisans as fabricators." •

A True City Abode
Jodie Patterson

BROOKLYN, NEW YORK, USA

ABOVE
A miniature Senegalese basket made from dried grass and recycled plastic sits atop books in the sitting room.

JODIE PATTERSON IS an author, gender equality activist, mother of five, entrepreneur, and world traveler, so it's very fitting that her personal style would reflect all the hats that she so glamorously wears. Jodie and I were neighbors in Bedford-Stuyvesant, a historically Black neighborhood in central Brooklyn with some of the world's most enviable brownstones. Born and raised on the Upper West Side in Manhattan, with family ties stretching from Atlanta to Accra to Zurich, Jodie draws her inspiration from a wide range of identities. She is also no stranger to fashion and styling, having worked in public relations for top global designers, and has an eye for curating the best looks.

I joined Jodie on a cozy February morning, just a few weeks after she moved into a new home with three of her five children (two are adults and leading their own independent lives). Having spent time in Jodie's first Brooklyn home many years and moves ago, I can't help but sense the same feeling that greeted me in her home then: There's order, but not constraint. Maybe it's more of a rhythm. There are beautiful, collected things, but they're passed down, used, and loved.

Jodie's eclectic and intentional sense of style is very clear, and she laughs at how "it follows me wherever I dwell, and I've moved around a lot—nineteen times in twenty-five years.

"I like my spaces, whether it's a modern structure or an old pre-war space, to show history, in particular the history of Black people and women. In every corner of every room, I have art that comes from the African diaspora, and most of it is livable, usable art, like stools, bowls, and fabrics. My design philosophy is 'build a home that makes you ponder about the people who came before you, so that you're inspired to do great things in your lifetime.'"

Jodie coordinates this vintage mirror with modern furniture and African accents. The tablecloth is a blend of indigo-style dyeing popular in Mali and the neon embroidered accents popular in Baulé textiles.

"To me, each piece says,
'We are not new.
We are not alone.'"

TIP
Use a textile, such as this indigo throw, to quickly add visual interest to a plain table. **∧**

PREVIOUS SPREAD
Jodie uses rugs, arts, and thoughtful seating arrangements to create zones in her renovated open-floorplan brownstone.

OPPOSITE
Every vantage point is an opportunity to add a decorative element to your home. Jodie introduces whimsy to the basement stairwell with a hand-painted wood panel from Ghana. Midground: a Quranic school board from Harar, Ethiopia.

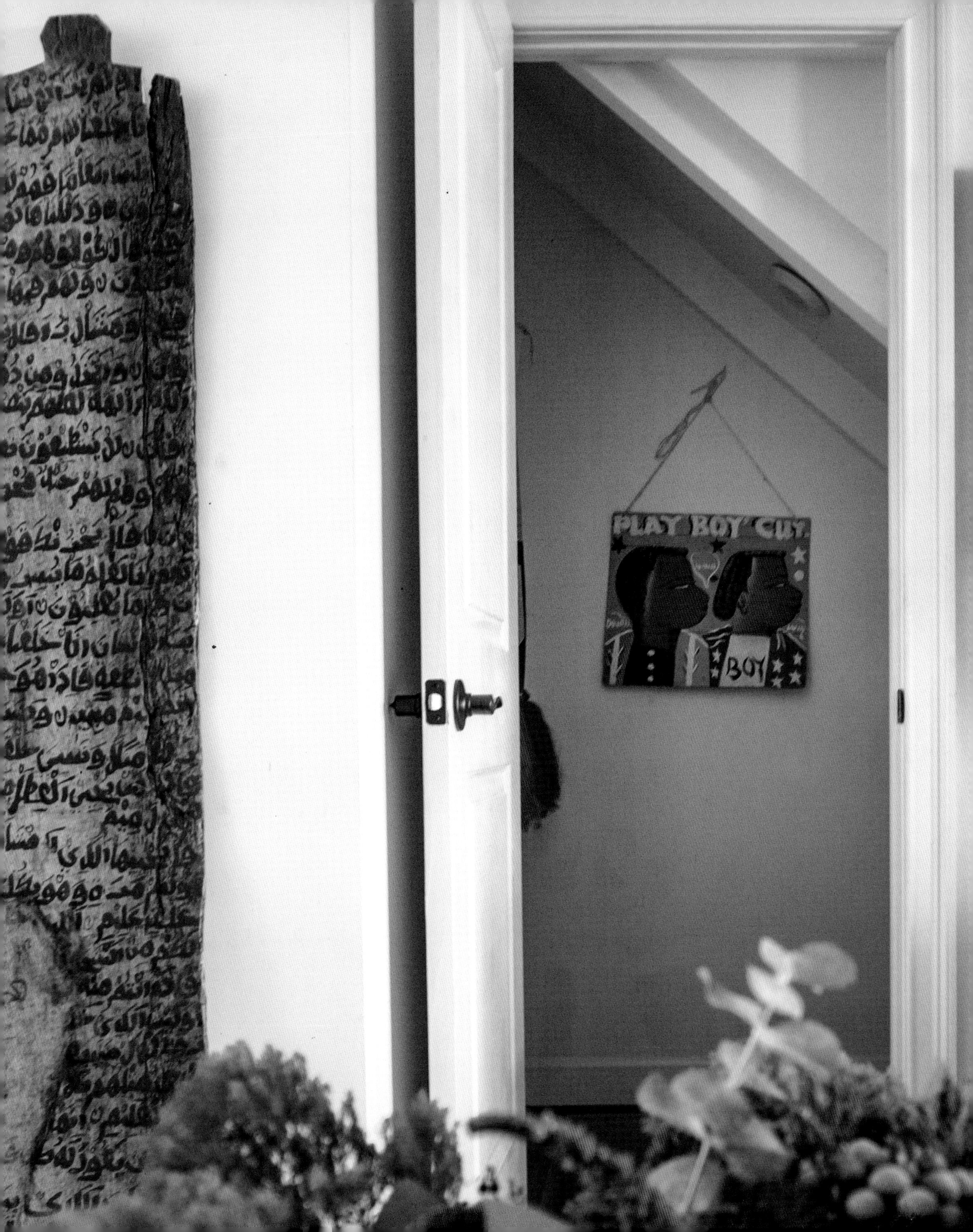
PLAY BOY CUT
BOY

LEFT
In the reception area, Jodie pairs a Moroccan rug with a vintage mid-century credenza. A Moroccan basket echoes the vibrant colors of the rug.

OPPOSITE
A small Ethiopian Coptic chair can become a stylish respite within arm's reach (and a rough-hewn Tonga stool from Zambia/Zimbabwe is useful to access anything out-of-reach).

Her style is informed by her background. "Back in the 1970s, my parents owned a private school in Harlem, and they collected beautiful art pieces for the school as well as for our home. Some of those pieces I still have. It's what I've always gravitated toward. And although I've lived in many different types of spaces, from lofts in Soho to brownstones in Brooklyn, my style remains 'actively Black.' Like, the music we listen to, the books all around the house, the paintings and sculptures—they all tell a story of my family and my people. As soon as you walk in my front door, you know the deal!

"One of my favorite pieces is the small gold-dusted figurine that sits on my dresser. She's so delicate, but clearly she's also so strong . . . withstanding hundreds of years and countless homes. In the same way, I love the beaded South African twins, and the miniature brass leopards. These pieces are all in my bedroom; I wake up to them every day, and they make me think of my parents. Then there's the round stool I use to reach high places in the kitchen. And the wooden sitting chair I find myself in while scrolling. I adore them all!"

As a collector, Jodie is a fan of travel, flea markets, and vintage stores. "I don't have a favorite place, per se. But wherever I go I look for something off the beaten path to find gems that fit my budget.

"The key thing is to decide on the mood or an idea you want your home to embody and then bring in pieces that express that idea. For me, I like to tell stories, I'm a storyteller, so all of my pieces give the evolution of people both past, present, and imaginary.

"If we could understand art as an intimate and essential part of life, we could live a more beautiful existence. African art and objects keep me present in the moment and teach me to remember. To me, each piece says, 'We are not new. We are not alone.'" ●

TIPS

Pair a Ugandan basket
with other wares such as
an acacia wooden bowl
to accommodate all your
fruits and vegetables.

<

A vintage Aso-Oke textile
from the Yoruba people of
Nigeria, Benin, and Togo
doubles as a throw blanket.

v

A Gallerist-Chic Apartment
Anahita Sadighi

BERLIN, GERMANY

PREVIOUS PAGE
A gallerist by profession, Anahita mixes several design styles to achieve a sophisticated and cohesive look in her Berlin apartment.

LEFT
Instantly "upholster" an ordinary bench with an African textile, such as the Baulé cloth in this entryway.

RIGHT
A small Kuba cloth mat softens the curves of this modern side chair.

ABOVE
A large Bedu plank mask commands the eye and anchors the room's charactertistically high altbau ceiling.

BERLIN IS A CROSSROADS, brimming
with artist, musician, and immigrant communities.
It is also the place Anahita Sadighi calls home.
Anahita seamlessly blends East Asian, Persian, and
African art in her unique, loft-like home. Her style
proves—as with so many traditional art forms—that
the commonalities are abundant once you pull back
the layers.

Anahita's harmonious living space is in the art
enclave of Charlottenburg. Steps from the antiquar-
ian bookstores and the Deutsche Oper, her top floor
apartment crowns this corner building replete with
post-war details. Step inside and you immediately
see how she honors the integrity of the architecture
while adorning her space with pieces from all
over the world.

This curation is Anahita's vocation (she owns a
gallery on the street level of her building)and passion.

"There is always a story that the artwork tells
and makes it so appealing to me. The contemporary
works, for example, are often by artists I have worked
with or know personally. Overall, I look for versatility in my collection, to be inspired by the work of
different cultures. The works in my home collection
come from many different cultural backgrounds. It
is a special concern of mine to preserve this cultural
diversity for the next generation.

"My living space is indeed always in flux. In a
way, this also applies to me and my work as a gallerist and cultural creator. Above all, it's important
that one's home is interwoven with one's own history, experiences, and individual lifestyle. My first
art objects were old Persian nomadic carpets and
abstract paintings by my father Hamid S. Neiriz.
An African mask from the Congo was also one of
my first art objects.

ABOVE
*Appliqued Kuba cloth is ideal for pillows due
to its softer woven texture. Consider adding a
panel to embellish standard bed linens.*

TIP

Dress up a table when it is not in use. Here, an intricate Kuba cloth skirt with applique and embroidered cowry shells is on display (although it is not practical as a tablecloth for dining).

>

LEFT
Another Kuba cloth panel accents the piano.

BELOW
Three African masks adorn the dining area console.

This curation is Anahita's vocation *(she owns a gallery on the street level of her building)* and passion.

"One of my absolute favorite objects is a female Bedu mask from the Bondoukou region (Côte d'Ivoire). Bedu masks were made by the Nafana, Kulango, and Degha tribes. They are usually made in pairs, female and male. The Bedu masks have generally protective properties, and the ideas that accompany the use of the Bedus, such as fertility and health, illustrate the special importance for women. I would like to keep this talisman forever.

"These artifacts carry so much power, energy, and emotion, and satisfy deeply rooted psychological needs. If you follow the campaigns in relevant interior magazines, everything appears almost the same: nude and minimalist, there is little variety and creativity. The world is so much bigger and more exciting, and African art plays an important role in the development of modernity. I am infinitely grateful to have come into contact with this world and to be able to carry and preserve this cultural heritage. The aura and history that emanated from the objects enchant my home and at the same time give me a sense of strength and rootedness." ●

"The world is so much bigger and more exciting, and African art plays an important role in the development of modernity."

———

TIPS

Layer textures. The coarse low-pile raffia of this Showa Kuba cloth is what gives it its nickname: African "velvet." **∧**

Consider adding a Kuba textile panel to your standard bed linen repertoire.

>

RIGHT AND OPPOSITE
Seen here with vintage East Asian paintings and tapestries, Kuba textiles' minimalist nature complements other artistic genres well.

Historic Oaklawn
Park Ranch
TaLaya and Kerrick

CHARLOTTE,
NORTH CAROLINA, USA

OPPOSITE
*TaLaya with her pup Honey,
whom her mail carrier and
Instagram followers are already
well acquainted with.*

ABOVE
The family's decor preference skews minimal.

TIP
Create a window treatment with curtain rod clip rings and an African textile, such as this piece of white mudcloth. **∨**

THE HISTORIC OAKLAWN PARK neighborhood in Charlotte, North Carolina, is unique: It was established in 1955 specifically for African-American families (both out of segregation and urban renewal). TaLaya, Kerrick, and their sweet pup, Honey, call this neighborhood home. Kerrick's grandparents built their ranch-style brick home in 1956. But when TaLaya and Kerrick inherited it and began converting the dated interior, there were a few design themes that remained central: an assortment of DIYs and authentic African objects. There's a very rich history that flows through Oaklawn Park, and they take immense pride in preserving the character that those who came before them worked so hard to forge. Their home honors history and intention through the stories the decor tells.

"We live in a small home, so function—and aesthetics—are both extremely important," says TaLaya. "Living in this house has challenged me to combine the two. In the beginning, my style was very colorful and bohemian, and over time, I started leaning into neutral color palettes. I'm a nail artist by trade and I create colorful art all day. When I come home, I want to walk into a relaxing home, and neutrals create that vibe for me. I still love textures and patterns, which I often incorporate using African decor pieces that I've collected over the years.

"Culture is very important to us, and being surrounded by things that remind us of our culture and our love for Black people was a very necessary part of our design journey.

"I've always been attracted to the craftsmanship and the details of handmade pieces and have always decorated with African accents.

"My Juju hats are my absolute favorites because they make such a statement and add a lot of texture to a space. But learning about their tradition is what really drew me in. And then there's mudcloth, another creative process that I deeply resonate with. Details are so important to me in my work, and I love to recreate mudcloth patterns on tiny canvases. It's one of my favorite styles and something that I am known for, and that inspiration came from using mudcloth in my home decor.

"Also, supporting Black artisans has been and will always be something that I'm intentional about. I care about where pieces are sourced from. I care about who my dollars go to because I want to ensure that the artisans are reaping the benefits of their amazing craftsmanship.

LEFT
*One of TaLaya's Juju hats
complements her neutral
living room decor.*

BELOW
*TaLaya makes room for
pattern in the dining room
with a mudcloth-upholstered
bench that she repurposed.*

ABOVE
Frame textile remnants to create a miniature vignette.

OPPOSITE
Create more visual interest by displaying Juju hats of different sizes staggered at different levels.

ABOVE
If you are limited in what you can affix to your walls, prop a shallow Ugandan ebibbo or Bolga fan on your open shelving to personalize your space.

TIP
Remember the hidden nooks. The artful placement of Ugandan ebibbo create a pleasing moment in this pantry. **>**

"In fact, being intentional about purchasing ethically sourced pieces goes a very long way: Learning how something is created, and the significance of it to African culture, is a way to really appreciate and honor the makers. I understand seeing something, thinking it's beautiful, and deciding to purchase it, but going a step further and understanding the origin and the process is a way to practice mindfulness and appreciation.

Also, amplifying and giving credit to the artisans through your platforms.

"These pieces are a constant reminder of our culture and of how amazingly talented we are as a people. The intricacies, the processes, the patience that it takes to create these beautiful and timeless accents is so affirming to me as a creator myself. I'm constantly inspired. And these pieces really make our house feel like a home." ●

LEFT
Dabito has documented his homes over the years, and I was thrilled to speak with him about his move back to his hometown of Los Angeles from NOLA.

RIGHT
Small stools such as this Nupe stool from Nigeria are excellent elements for curating shelving decor. This one was found at a vintage store in Texas.

Curated Mid-Century Modern
Dabito

LOS ANGELES, CALIFORNIA, USA

YOU'VE PROBABLY ALREADY HEARD of photographer and designer Dabito. You know his projects from their layered textiles and rich colors, memorable because Dabito does not shy away from bold statements. But his eye for prioritizing restraint through the use of dominant colors and color schemes (mostly yellows and blues) is what makes it all work. There's a certain restraint that one might consider a refined eclecticism, and his intentional panoply of pillows, baskets, and throws underscore that vibe.

A Los Angeles native, Dabito grew up surrounded by LA's natural abundance of plant life, succulents, and fruits. After a stint in New Orleans, Dabito returned to his hometown, and he and his husband purchased a 1950s Los Angeles mid-century style home that was not without its challenges. The sellers renovated it, and while the finishes were new, they were very conventional. But Dabito had a design vision and about 1,500 square feet to Dabify—his term for transforming spaces with his interior design skills.

The couple's new home is nestled in East Los Angeles on a quiet and lush hillside street less than ten minutes away from Dabito's family (so his mom frequently stops by with her delicious home-cooked meals).

The interior is a sensory delight that awakens something whimsical in all who visit, and the African objects the couple curate are an essential part of that joy.

Dabito notes, "I think it's important to learn about the rich stories behind the African pieces you're incorporating in your home. And try to source them from ethically owned businesses. African designs are beautiful and vibrant, so it's a great way to introduce colors and patterns in your space.

OPPOSITE
An assortment of Moroccan pillows and a Peruvian frazada create a true maximalist's calling card

——

"African designs are beautiful and vibrant, so it's a great way to introduce colors and patterns in your space."

——

THE AFRICAN DECOR EDIT

TIP

Fill the awkward empty space above a desk with a bold-colored Juju hat from Cameroon. ⋀

LEFT
Dabito was inspired by this basket gallery wall in South Africa. The pillows on the couch are Kuba cloth.

TIPS

Layer a plush Moroccan rug over a flat woven one to highlight each hand weave. **(PREVIOUS SPREAD)**

Place Tonga baskets flush to the wall in narrow hallways. They are shallow so they won't intrude into the walking area. **∧**

This bogolan piece from Mali creates an "upholstered" headboard. **>**

In a small room or laundry, substitute a Moroccan runner for a large rug: Your space will feel bigger and brighter (and they are also easy to clean). **>>**

"I began decorating with African accents mostly with rugs and pillows. On a trip to South Africa, I was inspired by so many beautiful designs—my favorites are the Tonga baskets. I remember seeing a ginormous wall of them at The Saxon Hotel in Johannesburg. I didn't know the basket origins at the time, but it made such an impression on me. I've never seen anything like it. And then the next day, while walking around, there was a woman selling the same baskets on a corner and I bought all ten that she had. It was kismet.

"I also have some special pillows designed by my bestie, Justina Blakeney, who has introduced me to a lot of African art.

"Each of these pieces are personal mementos. I sourced [many of] them with my husband, which makes them special and reminds us of our experiences together.

"I believe that decorating a home is all about celebrating your culture and identity. That's how you make your home personal and unique. I love showcasing pieces passed down from my family, researching and learning different designs from my culture, and then having fun curating them in my home." ●

RIGHT
Here, Tonga baskets create a focal point that draws the eye upward in a low-ceilinged room, making it feel more grand.

Near the Sea but Far from Home
Nina Mohammad-Galbert

TANGIER, MOROCCO

LEFT
Nina Mohammad-Galbert is the founder of Artisan Project and has lived throughout Morocco for over a decade with her daughters.

———————

TIP
Display a trio of pillowcases on the wall as art, as seen in this foyer.

>

NINA MOHAMMAD-GALBERT is the type of global nomad I've always admired. Born in San Francisco to Palestinian parents, she made a life for herself and her two girls in Morocco after more than a decade in Los Angeles. Nina is also the founder of Artisan Project. She spends weeks traversing the lesser-known parts of Morocco to work with independent weavers and to source ethical and authentic home goods for her clients. Since its founding, Artisan Project has worked with hundreds of women weavers and mountainside traders, addressing the common issue of exploitation by middlemen who often pocket the majority of the earnings.

So how exactly does one create a home *far away* from home? Nina demonstrates how she used African art and objects to transform her French Arts Décoratifs domicile into a port city oasis, in Tangier, Morocco. Coincidentally, Tangier has a special place in my heart—it is the very first African city that I traveled to. I was on a high school trip and Tangier was by far the most memorable leg of the journey; Nina's home and story remind me exactly why.

A lovely refuge in a bustling neighborhood at the center of Tangier, Nina's French Art Deco apartment building was built in 1933.

LEFT
Gingy finds a cozy respite in the den, which Nina decorates with vintage indigo from Mali, Moroccan poufs, and Bolga fans from Ghana.

———————

TIP

Moroccan bread baskets come in handy in the living room as multi-purpose bookends, and can stylishly store all sorts of phone chargers, pens, and little essentials. ∨

———————

TIP

It is important to note that many African rugs come in irregular sizes that aren't necessarily "standard" according to measurements in the US or Europe. For example, you likely won't find a perfect eight-by-ten rug, but you'll find something relatively close.

ABOVE
*The more, the merrier. Nina layers textiles and
Moroccan home decor accents in her home office.*

OPPOSITE
*Nina wraps a Baulé textile around one of her
many Amazigh capes.*

A self-described lover of texture and contrast, Nina advises, "Don't overthink interior design; rather, I just layer a room with textiles and objects that feel good intuitively. Rather than follow any trends, select what intuitively feels good to you. I want to feel uplifted when I walk into a room, so color is important, as is comfort.

"I've always loved African textiles and ceramics, so I always had a few pieces here and there in my living space. When we bought our home in LA, I started to add more objects and textiles; however, it was not until we moved to Morocco that I went

Moroccan wedding blankets, called Handira blankets, are made by the bride's family and grant the new union blessings and protection.

all out furnishing our home with strong African accents. The marketplaces in the Moroccan countryside are filled with them. One of my favorite finds is a vintage High Atlas Amazigh embroidered cape from the early 1900s.

"My Palestinian grandmother, mother, and aunts were all passionate about embroidery and were all very talented artisans in their own right. I, unfortunately, did not inherit this ancestral skill; however, I've always had a great reverence and love for embroidery. When I discovered the woven and embroidered capes of the High Atlas in a small shop in Asilah, I was instantly enamored and have been collecting them since." ●

———

TIPS

Moroccan rugs work just as well to decorate the wall as they do the floor. This style of display is common in Morocco.

The mirrored sequins are meant to ward off evil. These blankets are traditionally used in the matrimonial home as either a coverlet or wall decor.

THE ARTISANS

CAMEROON

Abdoulaye Mefire,
Bamum (Bamileke) Shields

Catherine Lontse,
Juju (Tyn) Hats

Honoré Njuchingan,
Bamileke/Bamum Stools

Cameroon-based woodcarver and workshop owner Aboudalye is an erudite craftsman who has translated his passion into a multinational enterprise. He is based in the Western Grasslands Region and supplies his brothers with shields that they sell in the tourist-oriented markets of Senegal, Morocco, and South Africa.

Catherine Lontse runs her Juju hat workshop and boutique in the winding alleys of a bustling market. She made a career pivot and started in this line of work later in life. She mainly works independently, but joins forces with other artisans when she (or they) have large orders. Catherine is a mother of eight and lives in Bafoussam, the capital city of Cameroon's Western Region. In photo: Catherine's studio.

Honoré is the head of a tight network of woodcarvers and artists in Foumban, Cameroon. He learned this craft from his father and has gone on to train apprentices in his community as well as at the Institut des Beaux Arts de Foumban. He lives close to his atelier with his wife and six children.

CÔTE D'IVOIRE

Abou Soro,
Senufo Stools

Abou lives in Korhogo's Banaforo neighborhood with his wife Yélé (meaning "first born" in Senufo), and their children. Abou demonstrates and communicates his love for the Senufo culture of Côte d'Ivoire by producing a range of Senufo stools, decorative objects, and ceremonial carvings.

Amani Christian-Lopez (Chris),
Baulé Textiles

Stylish interiors are made possible thanks to Baulé weavers like Chris. He has taught three other men how to weave, and one now works for himself in the small village of Aguibri creating the strip-woven and indigo-dyed masterpieces that the Baulé people are known for. He and his wife, Yaoble Gisele, have three children, ages eight, four, and just a few days old at the time of our visit.

Soro Nibé Salifou,
Dyula Textiles

Salifou trained as a textile apprentice under his uncle, who was a famed local master weaver in northern Côte d'Ivoire. He obtained such a high level of skill that he surpassed his uncle and went on to assume the title of master weaver when his uncle passed away. He lives in Korhogo's outskirts of Waraniéné with his wife Fatimata and their five children. In photo: Salifou's youngest children are three-year-old twins.

DEMOCRATIC REPUBLIC OF CONGO

Adèle Bope,
Kuba Cloth

Adèle is the steward of one of Africa's most recognized and influential textile traditions—Kuba cloth. She began making Kuba cloth as a young girl in her hometown region of Kasaï, which is the seat of the ancient Kuba kingdom. She is the leader of a women's cooperative in Kinshasa that specializes in the creation and preservation of authentic Kuba cloth production. In photo: Maman Adèle with a panel of Kuba cloth.

ETHIOPIA

Mamoush Gouzda,
Dorze Textiles

Mamoush comes from a long and esteemed line of textile weavers in Ethiopia. He hails from the Dorze ethnic group, known the country over for their fine artistry at the loom. Mamoush lives in the foothills of Addis Ababa's Entoto Mountains with his wife Maramuit and their two small children. He works in this community as well.

GHANA

GHANA (cont.)

Angela Afful,
Batik Textiles

Angela got her start as a batik artist while training in various vocational and domestic skills during her post-secondary education. As a leader in her class, she went on to teach others while still at school, and then again at the Kokrobitey Institute (where she was my mentor). Angie is a mother of one child and resides in the seaside town of Kokrobite, just outside of Accra.

Atanga Adongo,
Bolga Baskets

Atanga Adongo, affectionately known as Adongo, runs a workshop and marketplace in Ghana's capital city of Accra. He hails from Bolgatanga in the northern region, where he collaborates with other expert weavers to bring his original creations to life. In photo: Adongo (right) and his brother, Michael.

MALI

Boubacar Doumbia,
Bogolanfini Textiles

Boubacar Doumbia is a legend of sorts. He is one of the founding fathers of contemporary applications of bogolan, and as such, he established Le Ndomo cooperative to preserve the legacy of this artistic form of cultural heritage and expression. He trains young apprentices from all over Mali in sustainable bogolan production and life skills that allow them to earn a living as artisans. Le Ndomo produces bogolan for clients all over the globe.

MOROCCO

Naima Abekan,
Rugs

Naima Abekan is the founder and president of Cooperative Fadel Tighedouine, located outside of Marrakech in the Atlas Mountains. She founded this organization in 1999 as a place where young women and mothers could utilize their artistic talents for economic gain and independence. She runs the cooperative out of her childhood home and has added various work-dedicated spaces to it over the years.

Souad El Bahiz,
Leather Poufs

Once one of the first (and only) females dominating Marrakech's leather trade, Souad has been a fixture of the industry since founding her leather cooperative in 1993. She and her business partner, Rkiya, operate in the heart of Marrakech's leather district, where they make and sell some of the finest leather home goods in Morocco. They also export their goods to high-end stores abroad.

UGANDA

ZAMBIA

Agnes Musoke,
Ebibbo Baskets

Amissi Kyemo,
Woodcarved Utensils

Margaret Siansaka,
Tonga Baskets

Agnes is an experienced artisan and businesswoman who has made a name for herself as a basket weaver and community leader. Her home is a live-work space where she leads a collective of twenty women from the surrounding neighborhood who produce baskets for clients in Uganda and abroad. Her children, taught by Agnes, also weave baskets and continue the tradition.

Amissi represents the diverse and multinational nature of cultural heritage objects in Africa. He was born in Burundi to Congolese parents and has called Uganda home since his early twenties. Having grown up steeped in cultures that express themselves through woodcarving, Amissi continues this tradition and is one of the most sought-after artisans in Kampala. He designs an array of tabletop items and does custom millwork and carpentry.

Margaret is an artisan partner of the Choma Museum, a local museum and cultural center that promotes artistic education and cultural heritage. She was widowed at a young age, and this source of income has been invaluable to her quality of life. She lives and works in the town of Choma, with her son, daughter-in-law, and grandchild.

THE RESIDENTS

Nasozi Kakembo:
Maryland, USA

I run a multi-disciplinary design studio that fires my creativity and desire to make positive social change in different ways. This book is one of those ways! I share my primary home in Maryland with my teenage son, and I regularly gather design inspiration for my space and my clients when I'm traveling for work or for fun. I love to write, design, and photograph beautiful spaces and people. This is my first book.

Instagram: @xnstudio_

Hana Getachew:
London, United Kingdom

Hana is the founder and creative director of Bolé Road Textiles (whose Ethiopian artisans were also profiled in this book). She founded Bolé Road as a way to stay connected to her Ethiopian heritage while growing up abroad. She lived in London for a short time, but she is now based in Brooklyn, New York City.

Instagram: @boleroadtextiles

Nina Farmer:
Martha's Vineyard, Massachusetts, USA

Nina is a Boston-based interior designer and author who designed her summer home featured in this book. Her work on her summer home allowed her to explore another approach to incorporating history, one of her key project features, through her use of select African decor pieces. Nina shares her home with her husband, two daughters, and a host of visitors during the Vineyard's idyllic summer months.

Instagram: @ninafarmerinteriors

Renée C. Neblett:
Kokrobite, Ghana

Renée is the Ghanaian-American executive director of the Kokrobitey Institute (KI). She founded the Institute in the early nineties and has since relocated from Boston to Ghana. Sustainability and the preservation of cultural knowledge are at the center of KI's mission, and that comes through very saliently in the decor and design choices she made throughout Kokrobitey's campus and in her personal residence.

Instagram: @kokrobiteyinstitute

Emma Wingfield:
London, United Kingdom

Emma is the British-American textile arts researcher and co-founder of Five | Six Textiles, a social enterprise that collaborates with textile artisans in Côte d'Ivoire. Some of the artisans she works with are featured in this book. Emma has written extensively on the impact of art and design on global commerce, particularly in West Africa and North America. She lives in London with her husband Rick and their cat Jemima.

Instagram: @fiveandsixtextiles

Jodie Patterson:
Brooklyn, New York, USA

As a lifelong New Yorker, Jodie's international family and travels are reflected throughout her Bed-Stuy, Brooklyn, home. She is a mother of five and splits her time mostly between her primary residence in Brooklyn, her country home in upstate New York, and visiting her daughter Georgia in Zurich. Jodie is also an LGBTQIA+ leader and is the author of two books.

Instagram: @jodiepatterson

Anahita Sadighi:
Berlin, Germany

Anahita's home is a crown jewel in Berlin's chic Charlottenburg neighborhood. Located on the top floor of a pre-war building, she showcases her affinity for old and new. Her art gallery is on the street level of the same building. Anahita's family moved to Berlin from Tehran when she was an infant, and she has created an art-centric space to host cross-cultural symposia, poetry nights, and collaborative exhibitions that reflect her unique experience and underrepresented stories.

Instagram: @berlinartlover

TaLaya Brown:
Charlotte, North Carolina, USA

TaLaya Brown lives in Charlotte's historic Oaklawn Park neighborhood with her darling pup Honey and her husband, Kerrick. TaLaya runs her Artisan Nail Studio by day and is an interior design enthusiast by night. Her home is where she gets to express the latter; appointing it with objects that possess cultural significance is part of how she honors the legacy of her heritage.

Instagram: @ourbrickhousestyle

Dabito:
Los Angeles, California, USA

Dabito, affectionately known as Dab, is an interior designer and author who has embraced and popularized a much-sought-after polychromatic movement in design. A native Angelino of Chinese and Vietnamese descent, he and his husband live in East Los Angeles (and sometimes New Orleans—they're bicoastal). His style is defined by bright colors (namely, yellow), modern fixtures (some of which he's designed), and global accents.

Instagram: @dabito

Nina Mohammad-Galbert:
Tangier, Morocco

Nina is a native Californian of Palestinian descent who traded her Pacific homestead for one along the Mediterranean Sea. This is where she founded the Tangier-based Artisan Project, which connects groups of weavers and craftspeople throughout the country to individual and retail buyers abroad. Her approach centers each object's cultural value as much as its aesthetic one, and she expresses this reverence throughout the Tangier home she shares with her two daughters and her cat Ginger.

Instagram: @artisanproject

GIVE THANKS

THIS ENTIRE BOOK—and my own livelihood—is only possible thanks to the artisans I have introduced you to in these pages. Each one of our conversations have had a profound impact on me as a person. You have changed me forever and for the better, and I sincerely appreciate you for entrusting me with your story. Judith, you have been my co-captain and guide in Uganda for so many years—thank you for being a huge inspiration, motivation, and sister.

Thank you to all the generous family and friends (and new friends) who hosted me as I traversed many places I had never been before, and some that I was visiting again with a new purpose. Uncle Pit in Berlin—you always welcome me back with a fresh bowl of Liberian palava sauce stew. Jean Daniel, Manuela, and the entire Lambou family—thank you for your genuine hospitality and patience with my poor French. Thank you, Kiggundu and Herberti for being there with me and for me in Kampala and Kiwanga.

Thanks to Justina Blakeney, for reaching out to me in 2015 to feature some of my pillows on your blog, and now for supporting me in one of the biggest ways imaginable. Thank you for lending your wisdom and your words to this project, at various stages and in various ways.

Thank you to my agent, Kate Woodrow, and my editor, Shawna Mullen, for pushing me beyond my comfort zone and seeing even bigger possibilities for my work. Your vote of confidence early on let me know that we would make an excellent team.

Jason Reynolds. We've known each other since we were seventeen! Nobody could have told me then that we'd both be authors before we were forty. I mean, I knew you would be, haha. But not me. Thank you for the inspiration always, and for the guidance early on in this journey.

Thank you to the African Art Museum of Maryland and to Doris Ligon for hosting me during my research visits and extending your tremendous resources to me, both material and networking.

Thank you to all the friends who checked in and cheered me on in this marathon and were still there when I resurfaced. (Ashleigh! Love you, BFSR.)

I am truly grateful for all the photographers who accompanied me and/or captured the visual story in countries I couldn't make it to. Araba Ankuma in Ghana, thank you for providing supplementary photographs. And Amanda Archibald, thank you for my photography refresh before I set off on my own!

Thank you to my parents for stepping in when I had to travel during my son's final year of middle school. Thank you to my Mamas Crew at school, too! You all really held it down for us.

Last but certainly not least, a special thank you to all the homeowners and residents who so generously let me document and share their home decor journeys and other intimate aspects of their lives with readers all over the world. There would be no *African Decor Edit* without you.

ABOUT THE AUTHOR

Nasozi Joyce Kakembo

NASOZI KAKEMBO is a Ugandan-American creative social entrepreneur. She is the founder of the ethical home decor brand xN Studio ("Lifestyle—Without Borders") and the ethical sourcing consultancy Artisan Advisory Group.

She's spent her entire life at the intersection of cultures and countries, and her diverse pursuits are an authentic reflection of this upbringing. She was born to a Ugandan father and a Black American mother who met in Germany in the 1980s, where they lived for five and twenty years, respectively. She vividly recalls growing up in a household where African, American, and German traditions were fluidly observed, including the preservation of the very modernist German aesthetic that her mother had adopted while living there.

She obtained her first degree in art history with a focus on African art from the University of Maryland and went on to earn her master of science in urban planning with a concentration in international development from Columbia University's Graduate School of Architecture, Planning, and Preservation. She also took a semester of architecture at Catholic University in Washington, D.C. This educational background, combined with her art-filled upbringing, lends itself well to her keen understanding of—and commitment to—telling the full and colorful stories of the international partners she works with.

Nasozi has traveled to more than forty countries, including most of the countries featured in *The African Decor Edit*. Through all her journeys, including those outside of Africa, she connects with the artisan and creative communities who are preserving artistic traditions and/or creating new ones.

Nasozi is a board member of Mukono Foundation, a charitable foundation that supports primary education, arts, and culture in Uganda in the communities where xN Studio artisan partners are based. She splits her time between her home outside of Washington, D.C., and her homes in Uganda.

Credits

All photography, art direction, and styling by Nasozi Kakembo, except where noted below.

ARTISAN AND OBJECT PROFILES:

Morocco: *photography by Kirth Bobb*

Uganda: *photos on pages 44, 48 (images on left) by Mash Mugabe*

Ethiopia: *photography by Abinet Teshome and Sehin Tewabe*

Ghana (Bolga baskets): *photography by Morris Frimpong*

Ghana (Batik) and Renée portraits: *photos on pages 91 (top), 164, 247 by Araba Ankuma*

Mali: *photography by Tiécoura Ndaou*

Democratic Republic of Congo: *photos on pages 100, 102, 104 by Thomas Freteur; image of Kuba king on the throne, page 103, by Carol Beckwith and Angela Fisher*

Côte d'Ivoire: *photography by Emma Wingfield*

RESIDENCE TOURS:

Hana Getachew, London: *photography by Olly Gordon*

Dabito, Los Angeles: *photography by Dabito, photo-editing by Nasozi Kakembo*

Emma Wingfield, London: *photography by Emma Wingfield, photo-editing by Nasozi Kakembo*

TaLaya Brown, Charlotte: *photography by TaLaya Brown, photo-editing by Nasozi Kakembo*

Nina Farmer, Martha's Vineyard: *photography by Eric Roth, courtesy of Nina Farmer Interiors*

Nina Mohammad-Galbert, Tangier: *photography by Nina Mohamed, photo-editing by Nasozi Kakembo*

ADDITIONAL ART CREDITS:

Pages 126, 162: Stealing Stars *and cow painting by Traeger di Pietro*

Pages 198, 202–203: *Artwork above console by Daniel Butcher*

Page 202: *Artwork above piano by Hamid Sadighi Neiriz*

Page 187: *Ella Fitzgerald portrait by Amir Lyles*

Page 187: *Woman in beret by Essie*

Page 130: Tear for Biko *by Renée Neblett*

Pages 2, 128: *"You Are Magic" pennant by Rayo and Honey*

Artisan map designer: *Folashadé Akanbi*

Studio assistant: *Rosa Nomvuyo Filha*

Art direction intern: *Rafa Kalungi Kakembo-Swaby*

Editor: Shawna Mullen
Designer: Arsh Raziuddin
Design Manager: Jenice Kim
Managing Editor: Logan Hill
Production Manager: Anet Sirna-Bruder

Library of Congress Control Number: 2024933740

ISBN: 978-1-4197-6823-1
eISBN: 979-8-88707-040-7

Text copyright © 2024 Nasozi Kakembo
Principal photography by Nasozi Kakembo. See page 255 for additional photo and art credits.

Cover © 2024 Abrams

Published in 2024 by Abrams, an imprint of ABRAMS. All rights reserved. No portion of this book may be reproduced, stored in a retrieval system, or transmitted in any form or by any means, mechanical, electronic, photocopying, recording, or otherwise, without written permission from the publisher.

Printed and bound in China
10 9 8 7 6 5 4 3 2 1

Abrams books are available at special discounts when purchased in quantity for premiums and promotions as well as fundraising or educational use. Special editions can also be created to specification. For details, contact specialsales@abramsbooks.com or the address below.

Abrams® is a registered trademark of Harry N. Abrams, Inc.

ABRAMS The Art of Books
195 Broadway, New York, NY 10007
abramsbooks.com